**Sara Jane Boyers**

# Teen
# Power
# Politics

## Make Yourself Heard

Twenty-First Century Books

*Brookfield, Connecticut*

Published by Twenty-First Century Books
A Division of The Millbrook Press, Inc.
2 Old New Milford Road
Brookfield, Connecticut 06804
www.millbrookpress.com

Library of Congress Cataloging-in-Publication Data
Boyers, Sara Jane.
Teen power politics: make yourself heard/Sara Jane Boyers.
p. cm.
Includes bibliographical references and index.
ISBN 0-7613-1307-9 (lib. binding)
1. Youth–United States–Political activity.  2. Voting–United States
3. Elections–United States.  I. Title.
HQ799.2.P6B69 2000
323′ 042′ 0834–dc21          99-052192

Cover photographs courtesy RubberBall Productions, Orem, UT,
www.rubberball.com.

COVER AND TEXT DESIGN BY JOY CHU
54321

To my son, Morgan, age 17,

who has been political since forever

and whose perceptive questions

after a recent election

inspired me to write this book.


To my daughter, Kate, age 14,

her best friends, Janine and Elise,

and all other teens

with such great, fresh,

and powerful voices

that I feel our country

is going to continue to be

in good hands.

# Acknowledgments

Many people and organizations have helped me with this book.

From the world of politics, I would like to thank Lara Bergtholdt, former director of the Hollywood Women's Political Committee, who provided me with many contacts and engaged me in thoughtful discussions; Jeff Ayeroff, law-school classmate, fellow music-industry denizen, and one of Rock The Vote's founders, for his interest and advice; Rock the Vote for their suggestions and effective approach to youth and politics which I have tried to emulate; Gloria Kirschner, founder of the National Parent/Student Mock Elections, who happily supplied me with whatever I requested and offered even more; KidsVoting, with so many interesting teens; and many members of the Republican and Democratic National Committees, who always ensured I received answers.

Many agencies have been helpful, but I would particularly like to thank Kim Sutton, director of Special Projects for the Texas Secretary of State, whose Project V.O.T.E. curriculum is outstanding and whose readiness to answer my questions from the beginning of my research on has been most appreciated. A.T. Birmingham-Young and The Giraffe Project have been extremely helpful and full of good cheer as they seek out individuals and groups "sticking their neck out" for our country and community.

Jean Bethke Elshtain's book, *Democracy on Trial,* served as a major inspiration for this book. Edward Zwick and the Bedford Falls Company graciously provided me with show tapes of their television series "My So-Called Life," an intuitive take on teens which aided me greatly as I thought about what issues and approach to use.

Michael Dill, my favorite teen editor, took my request for comments from my target readership seriously and gave them to me—I hope I made the changes you wanted!

The students, teachers, and administration of Crossroads School for the Arts and Sciences, Santa Monica, California, who were kind enough to let me use them as a research and testing ground for some of the issues and ideas this book comprises.

Meg Blackstone, whose advice at early stages was most beneficial.

Faith Hamlin, my agent and strong supporter.

Jean Reynolds, my publisher, and Dominic Barth, my editor, who thankfully use email as much as do I.

My husband, Steven Boyers, who was relatively ok with the mess the house has been in over this long process, and who was always ready to point out current issues he knew were of concern to me.

And of course my children, Lily Katherine Boyers and Morgan Jonas Lambros Boyers, who never fail to demonstrate to me what teen power really can do.

ST 1982

# ontents

*I do not want a honeymoon with you.
I want a good marriage. I want
progress, and I want problem solving
which requires my best efforts and
also your best efforts. I have no need
to learn how Congress speaks for the
people. As President, I intend to listen.
But I also intend to listen to the
people themselves—all the people. . . .
I want to be sure that we are all tuned
in to the real voice of America.*

**Gerald Rudolph Ford, (1913 – )**
PRESIDENT OF THE UNITED STATES, 1974–1977
ADDRESS TO A JOINT SESSION OF CONGRESS, AUGUST 12, 1974

# Preface

As of August 1, 1999, the United States population between the ages of 10 and 19 (pre-teens and teens) totaled approximately 39,364,000 people, a hefty 15 percent of the "real voice" of America.[1] Yours are the voices both of the present and of the future. But are you being heard? For if your voice is silent, then your concerns cannot be known. With a groundswell of volume, action, and responsibility, together you can change the future – for tomorrow or for twenty-five years. There are lots of ways to do it. I hope you'll explore them with me.

*–Sara Jane Boyers*

## Chapter One

*Kids' rights will be the first to go. They don't vote.*

**Debra Hauser**
VICE PRESIDENT, ADVOCATES FOR YOUTH

# What's in It for Me?

WARNING
$500 fine or 6 months in jail or both for entering pool or premises when closed. LAMC 6344.D2

**House OKs Plan to Prosecute More Teens as Adults**

## School Disrepair:

**Many Schools Putting an End to Child's Play**

*View of Recess as Waste of Time Irks Experts on Development*

### Tired of Hassles, Skateboarders Seek Own Space

Banned from many parking lots and commercial areas, enthusiasts are lobbying for places to practice their sport.

**School Ban on Hugs Bugs Some Students**

**Students on Curfew:**

School Lunch Bill Leaves Out Military Children

Parents Vote for Mandatory Uniforms At Junior High School

**This school is brought to you by: Cola? Sneakers?**

Sure, schools can use money, but the ad business is going too far.

**Tax-free education savings**

**Summer tales:** Scorcher of a day. Air-conditioning's messed up and your room needs cleaning. Forget that. The park pool sounds like the way to go. Cool water. Friends. Grab the oil, towel, and you're off.

Hot pavement. Everyone's outside. Lemonade sounds real good right now. The gym's ahead and the shade looks incredible. You reach for the gate, but, hey, what's this padlock doing there? What's with this sign?

**POOL CLOSED INDEFINITELY**
**Due to**
**Budget Cutbacks**

**Fall tales:** Back to school. You're sort of looking forward to it–but wait! No backpacks allowed? How are you supposed to carry your stuff? Seems the school board and town council have been busy over the summer. When was the discussion? When was the vote? Who forgot to include you?

**Winter tales:** Horrendous weather. Stuck in school. Stuck in the house. Can't decide if being with your parents is worse than having to listen to your teacher's voice one more time as you eat lunch in your classroom. How many more times can you play that new CD? Only bright light would have been basketball practice–if afterschool sports hadn't been cut from the school program.

But hey, you're lucky you have a math textbook. Two of your friends have to share one, there weren't enough to go around. At least you can get your homework done without having to wait until someone else is through with it and you'd have to slog through the storm in the dark to get it.

*People who do not vote have no line of credit with people who are elected and thus pose no threat to those who act against our interests.*

**Marian Wright Edelman (1939 – )**
President and Founder, Children's Defense Fund

**Spring tales:** It's time to shed the parkas, bring out the camping gear, and get outdoors. But what are these buildings doing in your old camping haunt? Where are the animals that were in the woods by the clearing? What's this yucky red stuff running through the stream?

Does some of the above sound like what's happening in your world? Do you want to know when someone else is making rules concerning you? Well, if you do, then it's time to get interested in politics, the process by which you and others participate in making policies that affect us all.

People in our local, county, state, or federal government may not hear your needs as well as they hear the needs of those old enough to vote. As a result, if no one raises a voice to protect them, programs for kids may be the first things cut when money is tight. But the decisions officials make can seriously affect what you do whether it be how you dress for school, what you read, or what movies you can watch. In fact, by determining how much money or power to give to programs, our elected and appointed representatives are deciding for you right now some of the following issues:

★Where you might live (opportunities for your parents to work; roads or public transportation for commuting)
★How you live (minimum wages, tax rates and benefits, affordable housing)
★Whether the air around you or the waters you swim in make you sick (local storm drain regulations, industrial pollution regulations, spillage and sewage requirements, reservoir and water purification standards)
★Where you go to school (whether certain schools should stay open or be consolidated, public or private, in your neighborhood or elsewhere)
★Whether you have to attend school or not (educational requirements, truancy laws)
★The quality of your education (school budgets to pay for classrooms, books, teachers, janitors; repairs, access to technology, computers, cultural and sports programs, afterschool programs)
★What rights you have as a minor (the age at which you can drive, vote, drink, obtain working papers)
★The safety of your schools (open vs. closed campus, locker checks, backpack regulations)

★What you can read, write, say, print—and where (library restrictions, textbook selections, First Amendment issues, what you can and cannot say in student publications, artistic and religious expression)

★What rights you have as a person and a citizen (constitutional protections against freedom from discrimination due to race, gender, religion, sexual preference, and culture; free speech and privacy considerations; random drug testing at schools)

★What you can wear (school dress codes, length of hair, makeup, school uniforms, hats indoors, pierced ears)

★What is available to you for school meals (fast food in the cafeteria, who can get meals free or at reduced prices)

★Whether there will be outdoor/wilderness areas for you when you're older (ranch, farm, and land-development policy; wilderness protection bills, pollution legislation)

★Where, when, and how you can bike, rollerblade, or skateboard on public streets or property (safety gear requirements, quality of your public parks)

★What are your opportunities for higher education (college scholarship funding, tax allocations, student loan and work/study programs, affirmative action policies)

★Whether there is any counseling or help in obtaining jobs while in school or after (federal age limitations, summer employment work programs, school counselor budgets)

★Whether you can get to where you want to go (driving age, school bus funding, public transportation, road conditions, vehicle insurance)

★Whether a medical doctor or clinic can take care of you or your family if someone is sick or injured (insurance regulations, national health plans, hospital funding, HMO policies)

★Whether your streets are safe for you to walk, skateboard, or ride on (police budgets and enforcement, public roads and maintenance, local restrictions, crime bills, gun control laws, criminal penalties, curfew regulations)

★What music you can hear, movies and television you can watch, and Internet sites you can visit (local guides, government ratings systems, FCC regulations, ICC rulings)

★Where and when you and your buddies can hang out (law enforcement policies, right to assembly, nighttime, daytime, and mall curfews)

**Curfews – WHAT DO THEY MEAN TO YOU?**
**October 12, 1996**

MALL OF AMERICA IN MINNEAPOLIS, AMERICA'S LARGEST MALL, BANS KIDS UNDER SIXTEEN FROM MALL ON FRIDAY AND SATURDAY NIGHTS!!!!!

**1998**
Fort Lauderdale [City Commissioners] enacts a curfew for teenagers fifteen and younger forcing them to stay home from 11 p.m. to 5 a.m. Sunday through Thursday and from midnight to 6 a.m. on weekends and holidays.[1]

**Currently**
Cities throughout the country are enacting daytime curfews permitting police to pick up any teenager on public streets during standard weekday school hours. Throughout the country, more and more cities are looking at ways to keep kids off the streets as a way (they believe) to cut down on crime.

Back to School: August, 1999, Tecumseh, Oklahoma. **Lindsay Earls**, 16, high school junior, choir and marching band member and junior **Daniel James**, 16, both members of the Academic Quiz bowl team, have challenged the School Board's directive that all participants in afterschool activities be drug tested. The afterschool activities are tied to curriculum classes and valued by college admission officers, but students can't take them unless they're drug tested. Lindsay's never used drugs but knows that if she refuses the test, she won't get credit for classes she needs for college. In fact, she was already pulled out of choir rehearsal during school and made to urinate into a little cup in the restroom with a monitor standing by.

The Fourth Amendment protects us from unreasonable search and seizures and there hasn't even been evidence of persistent drug use in the district. The juniors feel that suspicionless drug testing is violating their rights. To ensure that others needn't be subjected to what they've endured, they are filing a suit against the School Board asserting that their Constitutional rights are being violated.[2]

Decisions like these are supposed to reflect what the citizens of the country tell lawmakers they want. If they affect you, perhaps you need to make your voice loud and clear enough to reach those in power, even before you reach voting age. Now, you may not know a lot about our government and it's true that you probably have a lot of other worries right now: school, finding out who you are, who is listening to you, perhaps a part-time job. You might feel that even if you could vote, what difference would it make? That needn't stop you from having ideas, from asking questions, from having the energy and the will to ensure that people listen to you. If you and your peers ask the same questions and support the same idea, if you send enough letters, politicians and elected officials will listen. You can make a difference. This is a democracy and you can let them know they are not hearing you and that what they do must take you into account. You're close to being able to vote, and their political futures depend upon you.

*I am particularly struck by the number of aged men who represent America. It seems we are not taking into consideration what is happening in this country today. We are not giving bright young people—who are often so much in touch with the time—a sufficient chance to break into politics and be heard.*

**Shirley Chisholm (1924– )**
**First African-American woman elected to U.S. Congress (1968–1982)**
**First African-American woman to enter the race for the Presidency (1972)**

Think about driving. For those of you who don't drive yet, your right to drive is only a couple of years away. Your parents know it too. They're listening to you closely to figure out what you might be like the day you take that f-a-s-t, powerful machine of theirs and zoom away without them. The right to vote slips up on us real fast—in most states only two years after you're eligible for a driver's license. Politicians, from the President of the United States down to your local city councilperson, are starting to listen to you right now. They are proposing programs that may not kick in for several years. They are thinking about the next elections.

They need to know–from your parents, your buddies, and from you–whether you'll be with them or not. The bottom line: you need to let them know how you feel.  Let's find your voice.

*Our society works life a café: All the citizens are the customers and the elected officials are the waiters and waitresses. Their job is to go to the kitchen (Congress, our city, county, and state legislatures) and get what we want and need. The problem is, many legislators have forgotten that is their job and worse, we've forgotten that we need to communicate our order.*

*It's like we go into the café and expect that the waiters know exactly what we want, even if we don't tell them. We see them bringing orders to others and we get angry that we aren't getting what we need. . . but we never tell them, and we don't hold them accountable.*

*Even if you don't vote, you still have the power and the ability to tell your representatives what you need them to know and should expect them to be responsive to your request. If they don't respond, you can always tell the people who do vote what happened and how you feel.*

**Andrew Lipkis (1998)[3]**
FOUNDER AND DIRECTOR, THE TREE PEOPLE, LOS ANGELES, CALIFORNIA

# Skateboard Tales from Oak Harbor, Washington[4]

**Sarah Swagart** is about to have a baby. She's seventeen. "I'm hardly perfect," she says laughingly. But life hasn't been perfect for Sarah either. In fact, having the baby is one of the least difficult things she's accomplished.

Here's another: On the Fourth of July, just eighteen days before her child's expected birth, Phase 1 of the North Whidbey Skateboard Park, the largest in the Pacific Northwest, is opening and it's all because of Sarah. But she's never been a skateboarder. She was a fourteen-year-old girl when she started this and they were all boys. She didn't know them and she calls them, "my little hoodlums." Getting confused?

Sarah's early story was about sexual abuse by a neighbor, subsequent drug abuse, attempted suicide and hospitalization, all before she turned fourteen. She wasn't your ordinary student and she didn't always fit what others felt they saw in her. When the community cracked down on skateboarders, threatening them with fines and jail time for boarding in parking lots and on sidewalks, she identified with them as kids like herself, "judged by others for the way they looked and the way people assumed they were acting—not for who they really were." In fact, the kids were "nobody special"—just boys who needed a

place to practice and show off some amazing skills. But the community called them "hoodlums." Sarah took charge.

She decided to give the skateboarders a safe place, perhaps the place she hoped someone would give her, where the "nuisance" level was reduced and the athletic and peer component of skateboarding applauded.

To get something done in a city, you start with government. Sarah wrote the mayor and asked him to create a skateboard park pointing out that, annoying as skateboarders could be, fines and sentencing were an overreaction. Recognizing that elected officials respond to their constituency (those who vote for them and those they represent), the next letter was to the editor of the Whidbey News-Times, appealing to the community— skateboarders and others—to help her get this going.

The newspaper letter and subsequent classified ads resulted in immediate response — the first offer to help from a member of the police department's Citizens Advisory Board. Skateboarders and skaters, also under attack; parents; other kids and community members followed. An architect offered to design the park.

Sarah formed "Nobody Special," a nonprofit group whose goal was to find a

safe place for skateboarders and change their perceived image in the community. Skateboarders and skaters joined in the work: obtaining signatures on petitions for land, participating in city council meetings when the project was discussed, and fund-raising. From car washes and penny roundups, sidewalk "mile of money" solicitations to formal requests for materials and construction from the SeaBees at Whidbey Naval Air Station, the kids are still working. They have raised a lot of money, but Phase 1 is only the first of the five phases and they don't want to stop now. Nobody Special serves as a clearing house for information concerning the project and has established a nonprofit bank account to collect the dollars arriving from the community for construction.

Sarah's past made her wary of speaking. She didn't even disclose her personal issues until she was sixteen. However, for Nobody Special to succeed, she needed her voice to be heard. With a petition for land in hand and leading a delegation of forty kids, she asked at a city council meeting why, if the community had baseball fields, basketball courts, a roller rink, and swimming pool, wasn't it accommodating this sport of choice for so many kids? Her powerful argument convinced the city to dedicate a portion of existing parkland to the skateboard park if certain conditions were met.

One of the main hurdles to approving the park was the question of insurance liability. If a kid got hurt doing an ollie, could the city be sued? Sarah's parents' phone bill and those of the others in Nobody Special zoomed up as they called friends and relatives throughout the country to find out if any skateboard parks were in their areas and how they handled insurance. This was "grass roots" politics at its best—the persons involved did everything to accomplish what they wanted.

With perfect timing and in response to public concern that parks were becoming too restrictive, Washington State's legislature passed a law prohibiting people from suing for injury from their own dangerous unsupervised activities in a public park. Called "assumption of risk", this returned responsibility back to the citizens themselves.

It has been four years from the first letter to the Independence Day opening, a long time to keep at something, especially for a young girl with other issues and for a bunch of kids who only wanted to be their own type of athlete. They stayed focused on their goal, worked with others to obtain the aid they needed, solved the city's skateboard "problem," and gradually won the community over to their needs. They accomplished it politically—with negotiation, through government and through community. Now, they've given a message to others, donating their park (even though it was city land, the design and financing of construction was theirs) to the city so that other kids coming up will know that the community respects their sport and their talent.

The satisfaction Sarah has had in achieving this goal for others, the motivation that carried her through the process of public speaking and, "a lot of weekends spent with a bunch of hoodlums," has changed her life, keeping her out of trouble, and clean and sober for years. She's going to register to vote soon. With a baby soon to care for and marriage to the father imminent, she's looking at the future and knows it must include political action. She knows that what she has done has given her a definite and positive direction for her life ahead—not always easy, but definitely a direction.

## Chapter Two

> *Democracy is the worst system devised by the wit of man, except for all the others.*
>
> **Winston Churchill (1874-1965)**
> BRITISH STATESMAN AND PRIME MINISTER, 1940–1945, 1951–1955

# Democracy

People around the world live under many different systems of government. Our government is a democracy—one in which the power of the country is in its people and exercised by them or the agents they choose. It is a system where we can freely express ourselves when something troubles us and freely vote for those who represent us. It is where we continually work to make sure that it serves us all.

Historically speaking, the United States is a young country and our democracy is shaped by the many forces and cultures who have peopled it—from the indigenous Native Americans and Asian cultures, to the European explorers and colonists; and from the generations of African slaves brought against their will to the waves of immigrants continuing today. So, when we think about the democracy that was created for us, our Founding Fathers were right on track most of the time. They created a potentially strong system that, when working properly, does provide opportunity for those who seek it.

> *The beauty of democracy is that you never can tell when a youngster is born what he is going to do with himself, and no matter how humbly he is born, no matter where he is born, no matter what circumstances hamper him at the outset, he has got a chance to master the minds and lead the imaginations of the whole country.*
>
> **Woodrow Wilson (1856–1924)**
> PRESIDENT OF THE UNITED STATES, 1913–1921

Our Founders worked hard to provide what they thought were ideal aims. Look at the Preamble to the Constitution—the basic law of our country. It calls for a "more perfect union," the establishment of justice, the assurance of "domestic tranquility," provision for the "common defense," the promotion of "general welfare," and, most importantly, "secures the blessings of liberty to" us and future generations.

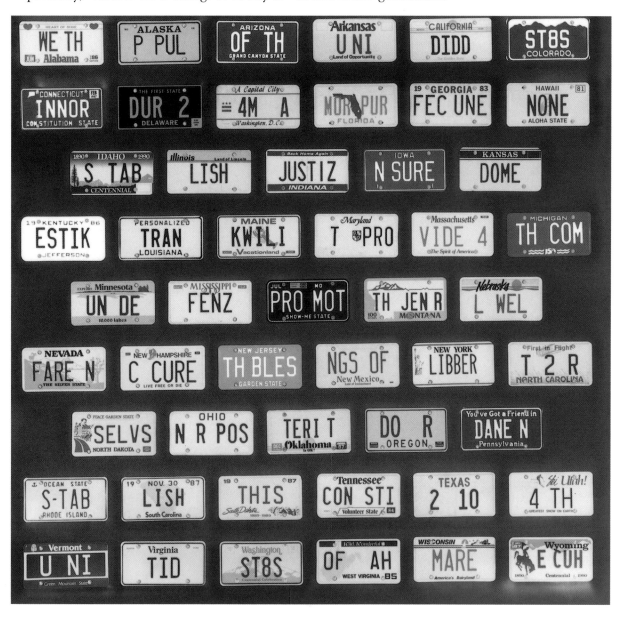

*In the long run every Government is the exact symbol of its People, with their wisdom and unwisdom; we have to say, "Like people, like Government."*

**Thomas Carlyle**
**(1795–1881)**
SCOTTISH ESSAYIST AND
HISTORIAN

In order to escape the perils of governments past, a government was created that could pass laws to serve all our needs—one of limited powers, with a system of checks and balances to prevent control from falling into the hands of one person or one group. Those protections are in the Constitution, especially the Bill of Rights, the first ten Amendments to it.

The Bill of Rights assures us that, "Congress [the federal lawmakers we elect to represent us] shall make no law which . . . " infringes on the rights of individuals, the right to a fair trial, freedom of religion and speech, press, and assembly [getting together]; takes property without just cause; does not protect the rights of persons who may be unjustly brought before the law. We were guaranteed the right to state our minds and to exercise our power through free expression and the vote. Of course there are limitations. Actions that work against the common good, like threats to public safety, are not protected.

SCENARIO

Fade in to darkened theater, you and your friends, just as the film is getting good.

"FIRE!!!!!!!!," someone yells! All around you people are jumping out of their seats. You try to rush out but the aisles are too blocked. Your backpack or bag gets caught in the crush, someone behind you screams as they drop to the floor to be trampled by others pushing past—and then, another yell, "Hey you all, just a joke. . . !"

"Just a joke." Right: A little kid's head was bashed in by everyone pushing and screaming, trying to get out of danger as fast as possible. Another broke an ankle as he tripped over others being pushed out of the way. Another is having a panic attack. Pretty awful stuff could have happened.

Free speech and freedom are free when used responsibly—another reason for government: to protect ALL of us. It requires certain limitations and this is the classic example used to illustrate when it's being misused.

As our democracy constantly grows and changes, new issues arise: privacy versus the common good, separation of church and state versus the common good, inflammatory words or acts versus the common good. As citizens, we must monitor the balance of governmental action versus the intention of the Constitution to guarantee us rights and power as free individuals.

There have been democratic systems before. The word "democracy" comes from ancient Greece. But we must work hard to keep ourselves free. All of us. And the best way we can do that is to use our voices and our votes, loud and clear. If we keep our democracy interactive, we keep it alive.

## Seventh Grade Tales from Sheboygan, Wisconsin[1]

Still wondering if your actions now can affect the vote and your community now? Read this!!! It started within the school, but teen ingenuity took it into the arenas of politics.

At the Urban Middle School in the Sheboygan Area School District, seventh graders, preparing for the 1996 National Parent/Student Mock Election, voted to create a "Promote the Vote" campaign, including creating a billboard to be put up several weeks before election day and several "Promote the Vote" video commercials. Contacting the owner of a local sign company got them a billboard free of charge. Cool! But the students asked, "Who would take us seriously if we didn't pay for the sign?"

With only a weekend to raise money, the students washed cars, held a school bake sale, collected and cashed in on recyclable aluminum cans, baby-sat, raked leaves, and dug into their own pockets, Monday, the students handed $111.07 to the sign company's clerk who was expecting to process a billboard order being donated by the firm's owner.

The clerk said, "I wasn't going to vote, but after hearing how hard these kids worked, now I'll have to." The company owner said, "I can't take the class's money but in their name I'll donate it to an elementary magnet school for physically handicapped kids." He also changed the sign's location to within two blocks of the middle school.

The local cable company agreed to run the student commercials. The video editor for the spots was so inspired by the student effort that he and the others at the cable station — some who hadn't voted for years decided as a group to vote on election day.

The local newspaper picked up the billboard story and ran it on the front page. Adults paid more attention to the campaign issues because pre-voter kids seem so interested. The weekend before elections, the six o'clock news of the local TV station chronicled the growing power of the student effort.

Schools. Parents. Business. Media. Community. All responded to kids like you. It was kids' effort. It was kids' ideas. It was kids' energy. It was kids' voices.

A successful project indeed: 84 percent of the parents of students involved voted (which, taken with the immigrant parents who could not vote, actually added up to a 93 percent total). Voter turnout citywide: 65 percent—up from previous years. Some 231 individuals contacted by the students (they also hung flyers and doorknob hangers) decided to vote who had not planned to previously. 100 percent of the students learned the power within them to make change.

NOW WHO SAYS YOU DON'T COUNT?

*No man is good enough to govern another man
without that other's consent.*

**Abraham Lincoln (1809-1865)**
PRESIDENT OF THE UNITED STATES, 1861–1865

# The History of
# United States
# Voting Rights

## Chapter Three

The right to vote means we have a say in this country. But free voting hasn't always been available to everyone. In fact, as recently as the 1960s, American kids who were not only major members of the work force but old enough (eighteen and over) to fight and die in wars couldn't vote until they were twenty-one. Where was their voice?

Our Founders were full of good ideas for the "common man," but in their day "freedom" and the "common man" didn't mean what they now do for us. Many were members of the middle and upper classes, with property and some education. They may have been European, but were now "Americans." They fought the Revolution because they didn't want control by a foreign power (England) over here. But they were not without prejudice. So while they gave free speech and protections to many colonists, the Founders gave the vote only to those like themselves—those they thought would be best able to guide the new country. In so doing, they left out many important groups but the principles they set into motion enabled those groups to eventually obtain the vote.

Thus, when the United States was first established, the only people who had the right to vote were literate,[1] white, Protestant, male, property owners over the age of twenty-one. More than half of the inhabitants didn't have the power to control their lives. This list included: women, Native Americans, blacks, although many of them were free, fought in the Revolutionary War, and owned property, servants, drunks, former criminals, Catholics, Jews, workers without property or education, Mexicans, Spanish, and French colonists as their settlements were not yet part of the country, the small population of Chinese. And youths.

Today these former exclusions seem an embarrassment. But in Revolutionary times even those eligible to vote had to fight for their voices to be heard. Luckily, the authors of the Constitution made it capable of change as our awareness of what we consider basic human rights evolved. And the fight for the vote continued, first in the newborn states, which retained much leeway in setting voter eligibility requirements, and then on a federal (national) level. Conditions gradually improved.

After the Civil War abolished slavery in 1865, the Fifteenth Amendment to the Constitution was passed by eligible voters in 1870. It removed voting restrictions based on "race, color or previous servitude." Now servants, some Native Americans, African Americans, and other people of color had voting power. As time went on, religious restrictions and property ownership requirements were waived and more gained the vote.

But in many regions of the country, public sentiment was still against giving the vote to the large African-American community. Although they now had the right and certainly the will, African-Americans were kept from the polls by intimidation, literacy tests, poll taxes (fees for voting, which many newly freed and poor people could not afford), and even murder. It took another hundred years to right this situation.

*The vote is the most powerful instrument ever devised by man for breaking down injustice and destroying the terrible walls which imprison men because they are different from other men.*

**Lyndon Baines Johnson (1908–1973)**
PRESIDENT OF THE UNITED STATES, 1963–1969,
ON SIGNING THE VOTING RIGHTS ACT OF 1965

Key years for voting rights based upon color were 1964 and 1965. In 1964 the Twenty-fourth Amendment, banning poll taxes, was ratified and the Civil Rights Act of

**AT LEAST 5,000 BLACK MEN SERVED IN THE AMERICAN REVOLUTION.[2]**
One famous regiment, the Rhode Island Regiment, was comprised of 75 percent blacks, including ninety-five ex-slaves and thirty freedmen (slaves who volunteered were immediately freed and paid full soldiers' wages). The Regiment fought notably and honorably in many battles, including the Battle of Newport, which General Lafayette called "the best fought action of the war."

## 2000, THE VOTE: A RIGHT OR A PRIVILEGE? WHOSE LOSS IS IT?

Crime is down for youth and up for adults. But adults keep talking about "youth violence" and they vote and kids don't. Legislators are proposing greater criminal sanctions for youth crimes, sometimes for kids as young as fourteen. Are teens to blame for society's ills?

Late night, Miami, Florida: Here's a cautionary fable based on several true incidents. Sixteen year-old **Alberto**, a high school student, was with some friends in one of Miami's urban areas. The kids looked suspicious and the police stopped them. Unfortunately Alberto, already on probation in juvenile court had picked up some pot for his friends and had it with him. He was arrested.

Sixteen isn't that old, but with consideration of the "prior", the Miami prosecutor decided to transfer Alberto's case to adult criminal court where he would be tried as an adult, maybe headed for prison. Pot's illegal and sales, even to friends, are wrong, but does this punishment fit the crime?

Alberto didn't have the money for a long legal battle, and in Florida penalties for felony crimes are serious. It looked better to "plea", admit guilt without the benefit of a trial where the judge could impose an even longer sentence. With a plea he might get probation and no jail time. What Alberto didn't realize is that time served wasn't the only punishment. In Florida, and many other states, conviction of a felony crime may carry with it a denial of the right to vote—disenfranchisement—and in ten states, including Florida, one conviction, even with only probation, can result in permanent disenfranchisement![3]

Alberto's not old enough to vote, and in a state like Florida, he's already lost that right for the rest of his life.[4] Not only that, a felony conviction can deprive citizens of important opportunities to participate positively in American life, including the right to teach or apply for college financial aid. And think about those applications asking whether you've been convicted of a felony! Kids just aren't being given that "second chance" which juvenile

*Without a vote, a voice, I am a ghost inhabiting a citizen's space... Before , I made my grievances known in violent ways. Today, what I really want is a politics free of meanness, a way to register my qualms without hostility: I want to walk calmly into a polling place with other citizens, to carry my placid ballot into the booth, check off my choices, then drop my conscience in the common box.*

**Joe Loya,**
DISENFRANCHISED EX-FELON AND PRESENT ASSOCIATE EDITOR, PACIFIC NEWS SERVICE [5]

courts used to give them and the stakes are getting higher, cutting into their most precious civil rights.

The media is full of stories of those in trouble in their youth who changed their lives to become positive contributors to society. Some stellar examples include: former Senator **Alan Simpson**, who as a kid was convicted of destroying federal property; San Francisco District Attorney **Terrance Hallinan**, whose teen fighting resulted in a court-ordered banishment from his home county; national weight lifting champion, **Percy Campbell**, a "career criminal" now planning to study physics under a college athletic scholarship; Kansas City Chiefs linebacker, **Derrick Thomas**, a founder of a reading skill program for inner city children and a powerful advocate for "delinquents" like he used to be; and **Jeremy Estrada**, former gang member and presently premed student in Los Angeles.[6]

They're the lucky ones as adults crack down on kids and build more prisons instead of creating opportunities for kids to advance. And while the change is widespread, there's no doubt it's happening in greater numbers to blacks and Hispanics in disadvantaged areas where better education, recreational activities, and jobs aren't around, but the police are. It's estimated today that 1.4 million black males cannot now vote (13 percent of the black adult male population!) and that as many as 30 percent of this population in your generation will be disenfranchised, often for relatively minor offenses![7] It's not only their loss but also ours as we all need to respond to the problems creating crime and we need to hear from legitimate voices of those caught within it.

Voting is one of the most important rights in our land of opportunity. Even if you'll never be arrested, do you really want to live in a nation where kids are denied their vote before they can use it or prove that they are capable of effort and change?

1964 was passed. The Voting Rights Act of 1965, strengthened in 1970, 1975, and 1982 suspended literacy tests in states with low voter registration and imposed further federal supervision on voter registration.[8] After years of protest against roadblocks to the intent of the Fifteenth Amendment, this series of powerful laws ensured that African Americans finally were accorded their long overdue voice.

Although some Native Americans were accorded the vote by the Fifteenth Amendment, most were not acknowledged as full citizens of the United States until the passage of the Snyder Act in 1924, although its passage signaled the defeat of sovereignty claims for many of the nations. Even then, several states did not accord full citizenship until the far-reaching effects of the Voting Rights Act of 1965 provided that indigenous peoples were finally secured a place in the country they had lived in before any others although efforts for dual citizenship or withdrawal are still proposed to secure better opportunities for Native Americans.

*Let me be a free man—free to travel, free to stop, free to trade where I choose, free to choose my own teachers, free to follow the religion of my fathers, free to think and talk and act for myself—and I will obey every law, or submit to the penalty.*

**Chief Joseph (c.1840–1904)**
Nez Percé chief on refusal to sign a United States–offered treaty in 1879

Can you believe how long before women gained the vote? Way into the 1800s, they couldn't even own property and were considered the property of their fathers or husbands. The mid-1800s birthed the formal struggle for women's "suffrage," the granting of equal rights including the vote. It was a fierce fight. Men, who opposed suffrage claiming women were frail and vulnerable, were not averse to slapping, tripping, hitting, trampling, spitting upon, and even jailing women who protested their unequal status.

The frontier territory of Wyoming was the first to grant women a vote under the premise that women, who shared the dangers and hardships of the "unsettled" West, deserved the right to be included in decisions concerning it. This "liberal" policy nearly cost Wyoming statehood approval. After generations of protest, the efforts of women and their supporters culminated in 1920 with the passage of the Nineteenth Amendment.

Twenty-one. The magic age. Or it used to be. It's thought that twenty-one as the age of "majority" originated in Medieval times when armored knights clanked around Europe. The armor was heavy and difficult to wear and it was assumed that if you weren't strong enough to hoist it on (around age 21), you weren't ready to assume the duties of a man.[9] The age stuck and has been used by civil and political society over the years as the age of responsibility.

Until recently, the voting age in the United States was twenty-one. But it is an arbitrary number and a lot is asked of youth long before they reach "majority." Even early in American history, people under twenty-one were working, paying taxes, bearing children, raising families, and fighting for the country. Gradually youth at the age of eighteen were considered adults in many legal contexts, including adult criminal responsibility. But these rights and responsibilities came about without the benefit of youth having a say with respect to laws that affected them.

In the 1960s, matters were brought to a head by the Civil Rights Movement and the Vietnam War. The growth of television and national radio made everyone more aware of national and political events. This nation's youth were seriously involved in protests for the rights of others. They fought. They were injured. They died. Even without the right to vote, youth joined together in a loud chorus and pressed for social change. By so doing, they successfully convinced those who did vote to make laws for the benefit of all.

*The reason the voting age should be lowered is not that eighteen-year-olds are old enough to fight. It is because they are smart enough to vote.*

**Richard Milhous Nixon (1913–1994)**
PRESIDENT OF THE UNITED STATES, 1969–1974

Republican and Democratic leadership and most citizens knew it was time to give the vote to this disenfranchised part of our nation. The Voting Rights Act of 1970 and the Twenty-sixth Amendment (1971) lowered the voting age to eighteen.

It feels like we've finally gotten it together and few are excluded from the vote. Subject to the voter qualification laws of your state of residence, the general rule is that if you are a U.S. citizen, you have the right to vote when you reach the age of eighteen.

With restrictions gone, you might think everyone would rush to vote. It's not happening. In the last few elections, less than 50 percent of the eligible voting population voted. An even smaller percentage of those aged eighteen to twenty-four are voting and they're the ones whose concerns are closest to yours.

# Teen Voting Record in Federal Elections since 1972[10]

NOTE: The "voting age population" is called "VAP" and for teens, consists of all U.S. residents of 18, 19, and 20, according to the census, whether or not they are eligible to vote and for 21-24 year olds consists of all U.S. residents of 21, 22, 23, and 24).

| | 18–20 YEAR OLDS: | 21–24 YEAR OLDS: |
|---|---|---|
| **1972:** The first time teens (18–20 year olds) could vote. | 58.1% of the teen VAP registered. 48.3% of the teen VAP voted. The teen vote was 6.2% of the total U.S. vote. | 59.5% of 21–24 VAP registered. 50.7% of 21–24 VAP voted. 8.04% of total U.S. vote. |
| **1974:** | 36.4% of the teen VAP registered. 20.8% the teen VAP voted. 3.81% of the total U.S. vote. | 45.3% of 21–24 VAP registered. 26.4% of 21–24 VAP voted. 5.88% of total U.S. vote. |
| **1976:** | 47.1% of the teen VAP registered. 38% of the teen VAP voted. 5.3% of the total U.S. vote. | 54.8% of 21–24 VAP registered. 45.6% of 21–24 VAP voted. 7.8% of total U.S. vote. |
| **1978:** | 34.7% of the teen VAP registered. 20.1% of the teen VAP voted. 3.51% of the total U.S. vote. | 45.1% of 21–24 VAP registered. 26.2% of 21–24 VAP voted. 5.85% of total U.S. vote. |
| **1980:** | 44.7% of the teen VAP registered. 35.7% of the teen VAP voted. 4.71% of the total U.S. vote. | 52.7% of 21-24 VAP registered. 43.1% of 21-24 VAP voted. 7.34% of total U.S. vote. |
| **1982:** | 35% of the teen VAP registered. 19.8% of the teen VAP voted. 2.97% of the total U.S. vote. | 47.8% of 21-24 VAP registered. 28.4% of 21-24 VAP voted. 5.91 % of total U.S. vote. |
| **1984:** | 47% of the teen VAP registered. 36.7% of the teen VAP voted. 4.05% of the total U.S. vote. | 54.3% of 21-24 VAP registered. 43.5% of 21-24 VAP voted. 7.14 % of total U.S. vote. |

| | 18–20 YEAR OLDS: | 21–24 YEAR OLDS |
|---|---|---|
| **1986:** | 35.4% of the teen VAP registered.<br>18.6% of the teen VAP voted.<br>2.49% of the total U.S. vote. | 46.6% of 21-24 VAP registered.<br>24.2% of 21-24 VAP voted.<br>4.73 % of total U.S. vote. |
| **1988:** | 44.9% of the teen VAP registered.<br>33.2% of the teen VAP voted.<br>3.49% of the total U.S. vote. | 50.6% of 21-24 VAP registered.<br>38.3% of 21-24 VAP voted.<br>5.56 % of total U.S. vote. |
| **1990:** | 35.4% of the teen VAP registered.<br>18.4% of the teen VAP voted.<br>2.43% of the total U.S. vote. | 43.3% of 21-24 VAP registered.<br>22% of 21-24 VAP voted.<br>3.75 % of total U.S. vote. |
| **1992:** | 48.3% of the teen VAP registered.<br>38.5% of the teen VAP voted.<br>3.29% of the total U.S. vote. | 55.3% of 21-24 VAP registered.<br>45.7% of 21-24 VAP voted.<br>5.87 % of total U.S. vote. |
| **1994:** | 37.4% of the teen VAP registered.<br>16.6% of the teen VAP voted.<br>1.99% of the total U.S. vote. | 46% of 21-24 VAP registered.<br>22.4% of 21-24 VAP voted.<br>3.9 % of total U.S. vote. |
| **1996:** | 45.6% of the teen VAP registered.<br>31% of the teen VAP voted.<br>3.21% of the total U.S. vote. | 51.2% of 21-24 VAP registered.<br>33.4% of 21-24 VAP voted.<br>4.4 % of total U.S. vote. |
| **1998 & 2000:**[11] | ?% of the teen VAP registered.<br>?% of the teen VAP voted.<br>?% of the total U.S. vote. | ?% of 21-24 VAP registered.<br>?% of 21-24 VAP voted.<br>?% of total U.S. vote. |

*"Don't Vote": This is an insult to our common sense, to two centuries of struggle for full citizenship, to Black efforts over the past decades, to become power players in the political arena.*

**Eddie Williams**
PRESIDENT, JOINT CENTER FOR POLITICAL AND ECONOMIC STUDIES, 1988

People in other countries look at us in amazement as many have only recently gained a voice in their own survival and opportunity. When the South African blacks and "coloured" had their first opportunity to vote in 1994, the lines for that first ballot were miles and many hours long. In their second election in 1999, 98 percent of South Africa's eligible voters voted. When people in Eastern Europe and Latin America first tasted the exhilaration and responsibility of an uncontrolled vote, masses converged at the polls.

In countries which are not free, the leaders depend upon the common citizen, and certainly the kids, to be invisible so that no one can challenge their power. Our democracy allows for all of our expression in our action, in our vote. Fight invisibility.

The death of democracy is not likely to be assassination by ambush. It will be a slow extinction from apathy, indifference and undernourishment.

**Robert Maynard Hutchins (1899–1977)**
AMERICAN EDUCATOR

## AN ENVIRONMENTAL TALE FROM HOUSTON, TEXAS[12]

Curbside recycling. An easy habit – separating trash and putting it in specific containers for pickup – that helps the environment. Seems everyone would do it.

When **Laura-Beth Moore** of Houston, Texas was twelve, she saw an Earth Day recycling demonstration that inspired her to write Houston's mayor to ask for curbside recycling. "No," said the mayor. Then, learning the city was to test recycling, Laura-Beth wrote again to ask if her neighborhood could be included. The mayor said, "No way." The test failed and curbside recycling was tabled.

Summer came, giving Laura-Beth time to figure out how to make recycling self-supporting and workable for her neighborhood. Not one for the usual twelve-year-old pursuits, she spent hours on the phone asking for recycling bins and recycling locations, even calling local realtors about vacant properties, often to be told, "Have an adult call."

The homeowners association, presented with a full proposal by Laura-Beth, voted to support a neighborhood program. Hearing her speak, a state representative backed the project. The local elementary school became the once-a-month drop-off site where neighbors drove their cars full of paper, tin, aluminum, and plastic, and teen

volunteers emptied them and loaded rented or borrowed trucks with the collected materials. Since Laura-Beth and her friends were still far from driving age, older neighbors drove the loaded trucks (the first rented by Laura using her own allowance money) to a commercial recycling plant whose payments soon covered the cost of the program.

The City of Houston finally caught on. When Laura-Beth was 14, Houston committed to a citywide recycling effort, having already acknowledged the neighborhood effort by sending two large collection trucks to haul the now 17-20 tons recycled per month. For Laura-Beth's efforts and research, the city made her a member, at age 15, of the Houston Waste Department Board — her mother had to drive her to meetings.

Cities throughout the nation will benefit from the persistence of this one teen as she completes and publishes a manual on organizing neighborhood recycling programs. Her community can show proudly how it

strengthened neighborhood ties by establishing a landmark recycling program.

Laura-Beth is now in college, the president of her local College Republicans. She's an active voter, aware that the elected state representative who first backed her made her goal so much easier. She wants to ensure that those who believe in her causes are those who remain active in politics.

## Chapter Four

# Why Do We Vote?
# Why Not?

The reality is that you've been leading a political life ever since you could talk. Every time you decide on something at home (bacon or eggs? which cereal to buy? which video to rent?) or you get together with your friends to plan something to do, you are getting information, debating an issue, and making a decision: taking a vote. McDonald's or Taco Bell? The mall, a movie, or roller hockey?

Political life is about getting things done, and, in a group, each will have an opinion. To get something done, you have to get information. You have to agree. Political life is about consensus—getting others to agree with you. It's about compromise. "OK. This time we'll see *Red Planet of Gore*. Next time we'll see *Pluto Slobbers Mickey*."

Voting is about exercising power and decision. It is an expression of our opinion and our choice. We do it all sorts of ways: orally ("All yays? All nays?"), by show of hands, by marking a ticket or ballot, and by standing in groups. We vote to get things done: by agreement. By selecting a leader to do it for us and with us. It is about being included. And when we're included, it is about participation. We have a stake in who's telling us what to do. If we don't raise our hand, we may not like the path chosen.

So why is any of this relevant since you may not be old enough to vote? Because your political voice can be heard loud and clear now if you want to convince leaders and voters all the way from your neighborhood to the White House that you are a presence in this county and that you have something to say and things that need to be accomplished.

## How Do We Make Ourselves Heard?

In a larger society, we get things done by joining in numbers to bring constructive comment and pressure on those who act for us. We select leaders to represent our interests because often we haven't the time or the experience to get what we need. They in turn appoint others to carry out the agenda they promised us. Are you in a club that has a leader? Who belongs? Who makes the rules? Is there one person who makes sure the rules are followed? Have all of you designated someone to act on your behalf? Think about it.

We make our voices heard by speaking out and acting to redress what we think isn't right through any rational vehicle effective in helping us accomplish what we want.

We make our voices heard by our vote to ensure that our government reflects our "will," what we want it to do. If it doesn't, we vote to register our complaint and to approve vehicles or representatives for change.

Getting things done is a continual process. You probably do it every day at home, at school, and with friends. When you keep checking in to see that what you want is being accomplished, it's more likely to get done the way you want it.

## Why Vote?

**We vote to make a difference.** Think about the changes you'd like to see. Is it better recreation facilities in your area? More classes you want at school? The lifting of the ratings on CDs? Internet censorship? If enough members of a group act together to make their desires known and get themselves heard, our country must act accordingly.

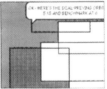

# Legislative Tales from Seminole, Florida[1]

Summer job at the car wash. Amid the humidity, heat, and sweat, **David Levitt**, sixteen, is called to the office phone. To his surprise, he is greeted by the flash of cameras, TV newscasters, and . . . a call from the governor of Florida. A lottery? No, David has won something much more important: a new state law making it necessary and easy to donate unused food from commercial eating establishments to feed the hungry.

It started when David was eleven. Inspired by USA Harvest, a program that transports donated food to homeless shelters, David asked his school if the cafeteria could donate unused leftovers to the shelters in his area. The idea had been rejected before, but David thoroughly researched his presentation: logistics, transportation, liability, and a packet on Tampa Bay Harvest, the local USA Harvest chapter for which David regularly volunteers. This time the school board said "Yes" not only to David's middle school, but to all of the schools in Pinellas County.

A 10-school pilot program was planned. But logistics delayed the start for a year. Among the problems: food packaging. David wrote Gladlock Corporation requesting help with the airtight plastic containers the county required. His request more than met Gladlock's public service commitment. Days later a UPS truck pulled up with 8 cases filled with containers, the first of many Gladlock donations.

The pilot program a success, the county then passed a resolution requiring local food establishments, not only schools, to donate surplus food. Interviewed by a local radio DJ, David was asked, Why not take it statewide? So he did. With a state representative's help, a 188 to 0 vote in the Florida state legislature resulted in a new state policy regarding surplus food donation. Then, in 1997, a law, written partially by David, was proposed, although too late however for the current legislature to consider it.

You've heard that line: "Good things come to those who wait?" Well, a powerful state senator heard about the project and, with his strong backing, the bill was revised. The Florida Departments of Agriculture and of Health strengthened its potential impact with their sponsorship. Next session, David spoke on the Senate floor, the first person other than a Senator ever to do so, and the bill passed.

The law is the first in any state to require that businesses supplying food commercially (such as hospitals, restaurants, hotels, and markets) make every effort possible to donate their excess food to agencies feeding the hungry. To make it doable, it provides important liability coverage for "good faith transporters of donated food" ("Good Samaritan" protection). A brochure explaining the law is now distributed when food licenses are granted or health inspections take place.

One teen created a local solution to one of our most pressing needs that could become a powerful national policy. It was elected leaders who worked with David to achieve his goals, so David can't wait to vote and might one day run for office. Right now, he's already working on proposed national legislation and definitely in the game.

*We are responsible for the world in which we find ourselves, if only because we are the only sentient force which can change it.*

**James Baldwin (1924–1987)**
NO NAME IN THE STREET (1972)[2]

**We vote for our future.** The generations before you brought the world to where it is. If you sit back, the direction is set. Sure, you're getting a free ride–but that doesn't guarantee the ride will be smooth or that you won't hit a dead end. If you're involved, you set the route.

For example: Those in government determine how the money collected from us in taxes will be spent. But government often spends more than it has and expects the next generation to make up the difference. Check into what government is spending now to ensure that you're not paying later.

## So You Don't Think You Need To Vote?

## Here are some of the worst reasons not to vote[3]

**1. "I don't have time."** Some effort is required to register and vote but registration takes about five minutes and forms are easily available. You do have to get to the polls (although soon there will be e-voting!) and honestly, to do it right, it's a good idea to study the candidates and issues. But think about the hours you will have to work to pay for college if scholarships and other student aid programs are reduced or eliminated because not enough concerned people voted for them.

**2. "My one vote can't make a difference."** In 1960's presidential election, if one more person had decided to pull a no show in every precinct (the geographic voting district where you live), John F. Kennedy would not have won. Did you know that one U.S. Senator won his office by only two votes? And only one vote gave Adolf Hitler leadership of the German Nazi party in 1923, dramatically changing all our lives. If you don't vote, your friend doesn't vote, and your friend's friend doesn't vote and your friend's friend's friend doesn't vote . . . it just keeps adding up. And subtracting from what might have been.

**3. "It's boring."** Lots of things might be more interesting than politics although there's plenty of drama and more laughs than you might think. And how much more boring would it be without summer recreational or school athletic programs in your area? Or, having to baby-sit your little brother or sister while your mom works because day care funding has been cut?

**4. "Politicians are all alike. They don't keep promises."** We put the politicians in office. We can vote them out. And don't turn off voting if the politician you adored turns out to be other than whom you thought. Another person may be. Perhaps you!

**5. "There are not enough African Americans, Hispanics, or women with real political power."** This is no longer (and perhaps never was) a Eurocentric country. There is strength in numbers and the numbers favor multicultural and gender representation. Barbara Boxer won California's 1992 U.S. Senate race because the state's Latino community voted large and loud for the first time and they voted for her. Although not Latina, Senator Boxer stood for Latino concerns, and together they could make change.

**6. "Politics and politicians aren't our age and aren't concerned with our issues."** Politicians act on issues brought before them. If enough of you make an issue known, they'll have to be concerned.

**7. "The system is a joke."** Fine. You're living in it. Change it.

27

# A Strong Voice and Action for Change

In the spring of 1998, 10,000 middle and high school students in the San Francisco Bay area cut classes, created placards reading "Schools Not Jails," "Stop Criminalizing Youth," and "Education, Not Incarceration," and gathered to protest, among other things, the condition of public education facilities in California.

Organized by the Chicano organization, Voices of Struggle, the students challenged California's funding priorities that allocated a 10 percent raise in prison upkeep but didn't change the education allocation. Students joined the protest to make the point that their schools had broken windows, no heating, and not enough desks or textbooks. Many school officials had to mark their students absent but quietly supported their strong engagement in the political process.

*Bad people are sent to Washington by good people who don't vote.*

**William E. Simon (1927– )**
**U.S. SECRETARY OF THE TREASURY (1974–1977)**

**We vote to preserve our democracy.** It's not perfect but the best so far in terms of letting us act freely and giving us the greatest opportunities. If you don't vote, you're not fully heard. And being heard is essential for democracy to work. In countries where rights are regulated by the few, the common citizen is subject to decisions they may not like yet, but may not have the power to change. Our democracy empowers us to express ourselves and to ensure by our vote that our representatives listen to our concerns and show it in the laws they propose and the policies they enact from local issues on.

For example, what happens when instead of your favorite pizza hangout, your buddies want to go to a place where the hamburgers are rancid? If you don't object or raise your hand to vote for pizza, you're invisible. They'll make the decision. You'll endure. That is democracy at work. This same principle guides our country when political decisions are made. People we elect make these choices. Pizza may take precedence now, but later it will be policy decisions that affect how we live our lives. Democracy is interactive and the keyword is "vote."

When kids make themselves heard they've done some awesome things. Even without the strength of the vote, youth powered the Civil Rights Movement in the 1960s and were the servicemen, the protestors, and the heroes of the Vietnam War. It was youth who marched into Tiananmen Square in China in 1989 to fight for democracy and who successfully fought in South Africa for Nelson Mandela's freedom and equal rights for all. And more recently, it was youth here who pushed our federal government to ease the often daunting process of registration with the "Motor Voter" bill of 1993.

Go back in history and you will see many instances where kids have cut through adult complexity and acted decisively and effectively. Even if you're not yet eighteen, you can still be heard in many ways. The vote will be that one last step to full change.

28

Before **Tom Richey** of South Carolina was even fourteen, he realized that he was part of a growing force of power and persuasion. Because he did the election homework for his busy parents, two informed votes were cast. By realizing that kids' political awareness comes from their peers and not from school, he became active in his local TARS (Teen Age Republicans) to learn the skills of politics. By realizing that he had more time than working adults during the summer before an election, he provided much needed support to his local political headquarters. Change can be effected in many ways.[5]

*In the end, we will remember not the words of our enemies, but the silence of our friends.*

**Martin Luther King Jr. (1929–1968)**
MINISTER AND CIVIL RIGHTS LEADER

29

# A Tale of a New Generation Taking Care of Its Future

## BOSTON, MASSACHUSETTS[6]

"In Massachusetts, there are about 400 beds for battered women, yet in [one year] alone, the Women's Hotline received about 92,000 calls from women requesting help or information." So starts the press release from F.A.S.T. (Friends and Shelter for Teens), the teen-run corporation founded by **Cecilia-Nan Ding** in her high school junior year. The increasing rise of domestic physical and verbal abuse—battered women, children, teens—made Cecilia want to reach out and activate teens about their concerns. "Teens today are not Generation X. I call us the "A" Generation, one that is new, fresh, and ready to resolve their problems right now."

Are battered women really an issue for kids? From F.A.S.T.'s press release: "Last year alone in Massachusetts, 900 restraining orders [were] taken out by teenage girls against their abusive boyfriends." Children and teens living in a situation of abuse know its power to tear families apart.

Only five years in the United States, Cecilia, an emigrant from Tianjin, China, quickly adapted to the American style of entrepreneurship. She formed F.A.S.T. as an enduring project under the umbrella of INA (Increases Your Natural Ability), a non-profit company helping teens start their own business. F.A.S.T has a twelve-year growth plan and formal structure providing for delegation and departmentalization. The first phase: awareness, research, and education for abuse prevention, teen recruitment, and legislation.

F.A.S.T. is totally teen-staffed and teen-run as high school students take ownership of their own ideas and push their own agenda, with adult support only when requested. Among the current projects:

**1. A strong media and outreach presence:** F.A.S.T. buys time on the local cable network for weekly issue-oriented programming with a teen perspective. The show includes local bands, media celebrities, and teens who speak about how domestic abuse affects their lives. Producers, directors, cameramen, and coordinators are high school students, honing their programming and technical skills.

Two concerts resulted in greater public outreach. Kids, national domestic violence groups, and elected officials are calling to listen to this potentially powerful teen voice.

The Act F.A.S.T Crew Players are ready to tour a play they have written about an abusive relationship. Their desired venue: Boston community youth centers.

*A Generation* is in development—for possible distribution in the Boston public schools —a newspaper/'zine with teen journalists in training, writing from their own viewpoint and style about local, national, and global concerns.

Their strong website is self-designed and self-maintained.

**2. Legislative:** F.A.S.T.'s legislative department has researched and is proposing two bills as a radical, creative solution for domestic violence. The first requires Massachusetts juvenile courts to hold parents AND the community jointly responsible (and subject to criminal sanctions) for the act of a convicted youth felon if there is evidence of "unhealthiness" in the situation. The second bill requires local government to provide a set number of shelter beds for victims of domestic and dating violence based upon the female population of the community or the frequency of hotline calls for a set period.

**3. Additional offices in the state, region, and nation** are expected to expand the mission.

Cecilia can't even vote yet—she's too young and not yet a citizen—but will as soon as she can ("After all that's what America stands for"). But she's already

working within the system to accomplish what the system hasn't done. With a business plan in place, department heads, recruitment programs, a funding and step-development plan, F.A.S.T. is raising teen awareness and advocacy through a company structured for stability, empowerment, and change — a new venue for teen voices.

## Chapter Five

*Su Vota es su Voz*
*(Your vote is your voice)*

**William C. "Willie" Velásquez (1944–1988)**
FOUNDER OF SOUTHWEST VOTER REGISTRATION EDUCATION PROJECT,
DEDICATED TO INCREASING THE PARTICIPATION OF LATINOS AND
OTHER RACIAL AND ETHNIC COMMUNITIES IN THE
AMERICAN DEMOCRATIC PROCESS.

# The Election Process

Take a look at the formal election process to really understand what it is. With the knowledge of what happens in an election, you can influence current policy and votes whether you are voting age or not.

## Whom and What Do We Vote For?

To get things done, we need good leaders and good laws. Let's discuss leaders first. Generally, their work falls into three main categories:

☆ **Executive:** to run the government (the president and vice president of the United States, state governors, and city mayors who are elected to executive office);
☆ **Legislative:** to pass laws (state and federal senators, members of the federal House of Representatives, state assemblies, and city councils); and
☆ **Judiciary:** to ensure that our laws are fairly exercised (local judges, justices of the peace, state and federal courts of appeal and the Supreme Court–some appointed, some elected).

# Teenage Pamphleteer Joins School Board Race[1]

**Basset High School,
La Puente, California**

The principal limits the school newspaper's scope after a senior student writes an editorial criticizing the decision to cut down campus trees. Outraged, the same student distributes a flyer comparing the principal to several demagogues, including Hitler. Seven weeks pass. Finals and graduation are approaching —the senior was to sing the national anthem at the ceremony —when the senior was summarily suspended, informed he would be arrested if he returned and would probably be expelled. The reason? The administration felt the flyer had created a "threatening situation" at the school, although nothing had happened.

Teachers felt the suspension infringed upon constitutionally protected free speech and dressed in red and blue to protest. The local newspaper contacted the ACLU (American Civil Liberties Union) which, just six hours before graduation, obtained a restraining order from the U.S. District Court to allow the senior, having taken his finals privately, to graduate and proudly sing the anthem in front of all his peers.

Concern about student rights led the senior to draft the flyer. Two months after graduation, at the eligible age of eighteen, he announced his candidacy for school board in the very district from which he had almost been expelled. His position: "Who knows better what students need?" Learning from his experience (although legally permissible, he admits he would have reworded the flyer), he proposed better communication between the student body, teachers, administrators, and parents in his district. He didn't win but garnered a respectable vote and the issues he raised inspired reforms within the district.

> *In our system, state-operated schools may not be enclaves of totalitarianism. School officials do not possess absolute authority over their students. Students in school as well as out of school are "persons" under our Constitution.*
>
> **Justice Abe Fortas (1910–1982)**
> ASSOCIATE JUSTICE OF THE SUPREME COURT OF THE UNITED STATES, 1965–1969
> TINKER V. DES MOINES (1969)

People drawn to public service give themselves over to representing others in order to get something done in a certain way. As our voice, we expect them to be in harmony with us. Why do they do it? The answer isn't simple. It probably falls somewhere between a selfless interest in the public good and an interest in their own political gain, which is okay as long as their career tactics do not undermine the promises made to get elected. Candidates who want your support can be professional politicians whose career is seeking public office again and again. But they can also be "regular" folk whose interest in helping their own community inspires them to enter politics. They can be athletes and celebrities who decide to use their powerful media presence to convince others to think as they do. They can be lawyers and judges whose interest is in preserving the principles of the Constitution. They can be moms. Or even kids or at least, young voters.

**We can't afford to sit anything out, any more than we can afford to have so-called leaders who sit and take it.**

**Paul Robeson (1898–1976)**[2]
**ENTERTAINER AND POLITICAL ACTIVIST**

We also vote on legislation that affects, whether new programs, new funding for existing ones, or new amendments to the Constitution. Proposed laws (propositions) are placed on the ballot by legislators and sometimes by citizens who have collected enough voter signatures on a petition to authorize its inclusion.

From local to federal if we see that voting for legislation or people will back up whatever else we are doing, but we don't take that step (voting ourselves or getting others out to vote), then things don't happen the way we need them to.

**SOUTH DAKOTA.** One of the least populous states in the Union. One where youth leaves more than stays. Their departure spells economic and social disaster for the region. How to hold them there? This is a question **Justin Kopetsky**, as a Student Panel Board member of KidsVoting USA, and a resident of Frederick, South Dakota (population 250)[3], confronts daily.

A high school senior, Justin works with teens around the state to develop interest in the political process and see why kids leave and how to attract them to stay or return. The answers lie in work opportunities in a rural agrarian economy and sparsely populated state. Even before they vote, kids in South Dakota need to ensure their state and federal representatives are on top of legislation providing for grain minimums; ranch, farming, and parkland issues with respect to the reintroduction of bison; international trade agreements affecting farm produce; funding opportunities for

school systems; or whether subsidies are available for start-up businesses to keep youth there. Other concerns: driving ages (in a rural state, kids drive often far earlier than urban kids do) and making the perspective of youth heard while ensuring they get the information they need.

Through KidsVoting, Justin helped organize a 22-state cyberchat between several schools (elementary through high school) in each state and two prominent U.S. Senators, one Democrat and one Republican. The leaders heard concerned voices from a population not always well represented in Congress and students were able to learn directly the Senators' views.

Justin is now known throughout the state, speaking at major sports events, organizing "Youth on

Youth Perspective" conferences, and participating in radio spots for voting PSAs. He believes that his generation can do anything and he is hoping to turn that energy to South Dakota's benefit. By participating in the national activities of KidsVoting, Justin is able to bring to the forefront the perspective of his small state and bring back to South Dakota some of the solutions derived from more industrial ones.

He plans to stay in the arena, studying political science in college and acquiring further skills to aid his community, state, and country.

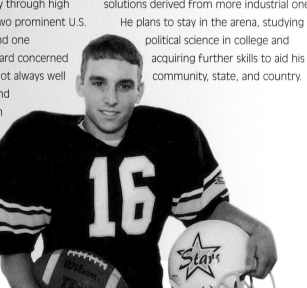

## What Types of Elections Are There?

**Local (city, town, or county):** We elect mayors, city managers, or the county Board of Supervisors; city councilmembers; the Board of Education; judges and sheriffs. We are asked to pass or defeat local issues which could include zoning ordinances, local roads, and school issues or whether you can rollerblade or skateboard at your city park.

**State:** We vote for the governor, lieutenant governor, attorney general (the legal arm of the state), secretary of state, treasurer, judges, superintendent of Education, state senators and state representatives. We vote on tax issues and amendments to the state constitution. The death penalty might be an issue we would vote on at a state level.

**Federal:** We vote for the president and the vice president of the United States, the members of Congress (senators and representatives), and amendments to the Constitution. (The Justices of the Supreme Court are appointed by presidents.)

## When Do We Vote?

Elections take place at varying times. Presidential elections are held every four years in years evenly divisible by the number "4" ( e.g. 1996, 2000, 2004 . . . ) on the first Tuesday after the first Monday in November. Other federal elections are held in even-numbered years, (e.g. 1998, 2000, 2002 . . . ). State and local issues and candidates are often included on the federal ballot.

Your state usually has at least two elections in any federal election year. The first is the primary or caucus, held anywhere from late winter to early October when more than one candidate from the same political party wishes to run for a bipartisan (involving candidates from at least two political parties) office or where there are multiple candidates for a nonpartisan office. It is held to determine who will be that party's nominee to run against an opposing party's candidate in the national election.

In general, elective office and issues are grouped together on one ballot, although varying issues may require another election. Your local

**"Me, me, me me me me ME!"**

election board may notify you of other elections held to elect or pass for example, a new school bond, regional legislation, or an elective office that may suddenly need to be filled.

Don't be fooled into thinking that presidential elections are the only ones that

# A Tale of Local Activism in Scottsdale, Arizona[4]

Sophomore high school biology. **James "Ryan" Mitchell** wasn't looking forward to it. But the surprising concurrence of an inspiring teacher, class choices, and civic circumstances sent Ryan on a journey that changed not only him but the life of his entire community as well.

The biology teacher was never in the classroom. But then, neither were the students as class was often held outdoors. Best of all: a 120-acre site, the last remaining piece of natural desert around. It was a magical place, where 110 species of wildlife wandered freely in a complex environment of varying biomes: canal/wash, wetland to mountainous (created by the neighboring development whose roofs became nesting and perching sites).

And it was to become a golf course, the contours already gouged into the land.

Ryan knew he wanted the golf course stopped and the area restored and preserved. He made saving the wash his project for his school service learning program, the National Youth Leadership Center (NYLC). "Cool," he thought, "get some support from classmates, get media down there, present the concern, and go from there." Well, yes and no. Sometimes things

get a little complex.

In response to his calls, the local newspaper published a front page article headlined "Wash to Go Wild?" Calls rolled in to the NYLC's little office, including one from the city council office asking Ryan what he was doing with their land. Oops.

While acknowledging that things might have started better had he learned who actually owned the land, as a result of Ryan's actions, the city listened. Eight NYLC students and Ryan held the first of many power meetings with the city: Three city council administrators, the director of Parks & Recreation, the City Endowment Offices, Maricopa County Flood Control, and the U.S. Army Corps of Engineers who had jurisdiction over the flood plain. Two newspapers covered the meeting.

Using visuals, research reports, and new political skills, Ryan made it clear his group was committed to restoring and saving the acreage for wildlife and educational use. Effective change starts by making those involved aware of the issues. Faced with the depth of the group's preparation, the officials realized Ryan was serious.

But when the adjacent housing development was created, the developer

promised property buyers a golf course for which they paid extra based upon city plans. The developer ran off with their money. A subsequent developer ran off, too, but only after tearing up the land and removing topsoil. Although advised that the project was too costly, the city still felt obligated to it. Saving the acres wasn't going to be easy.

After that first meeting, the wildlife park became a local election issue, affecting several city council elections. The owner of a 200-theater movie chain, presented with the NYLC's 100-page information packet, gave "slide time" in area theaters, $6,000 of free publicity. Other presentations to the school district, local business, and the Audubon Society garnered their support. Members of the greater Scottsdale community began to wonder why a city with thirty-two golf courses needed another. The *Scottsdale Tribune* conducted a call-in poll, "Birds vs. Birdies." The birds won.

matter because they get more press. Congressional seats are up for grabs every two years. Senators hold their office for six years and terms are staggered so that one-third of the Senate is up for election every two years. And Representatives' terms are just two years in length. State and local elections are held at many different times. Unfortunately

The students were empowered. In Ryan's junior year, the city negotiated, offering to reserve 20 acres from the golf course—those along the wash—for environmental and educational purposes under an IGA (Intergovernmental Agreement) between the school district and the city. Only 20 acres as opposed to 120? Ryan didn't want to consider it, but reality was setting in. The city was going ahead with the course and, while "shooting for the skies," what could Ryan really expect? Much of his group had graduated and the decision was his. At the next city council meeting, Ryan accepted a compromise and the deal was approved. "One of the hardest moments of my life" for Ryan, who was realizing that political gain is often a series of small steps and partial victories.

By keeping their cool while navigating the system, the NYLC project was successfully heard. Some had suggested (and the media was pressing for) more dramatic action, but the NYLC directive was clear: nonpolitical, polite, and no bridges burned. After all, the land would be subject to other municipal decisions.

For its work, the NYLC wash project won national and international awards, including a United Nations stamp of approval and, for Ryan, the honor of representing the United States at an international environmental conference in Israel. Inspired by the honors, the local power company worked with the NYLC to sponsor a concurrent exchange program (ten students including Ryan) with Israeli students whose country shares the Sonoran desert ecology running in a strip around the planet.

By Ryan's senior year, the wash project was set with student educational days, clean up days (local businesses donated equipment and employees as volunteers), and basic maintenance schedules. The NYLC also organized a 400-acre wildlife park on vacant land for the neighboring city of Tempe. Throughout the greater Phoenix, Arizona, area (including Scottsdale and Tempe), NYLC students are now working on saving and managing twenty-four sites, from large to pocket park.

The NYLC "gave away" their first project, the 20-acre wash, to the adjacent elementary school, where kindergarten through fifth graders visit every month, clean up, plant their trees, and learn about their animals. High school students teach them how to maintain the park. Ryan's Saguaro High School NYLC also bit the bullet and gave the 400-acre Tempe site to their rival high school. Ryan feels "the city had faith in us when they gave us the first 20 acres. We needed to learn to have faith in others, even rivals." Together and with compromise, teens and the city shifted course to enable a gain for all. The skills learned will remain with the NYLC group whatever they attempt. And the city now knows to listen to the voices of those so loud and eloquent.

For Ryan, "environmental stewardship" meant first educating himself and others in environmental and political activism. He's now eighteen and registered to vote, excited most with the local election issues upcoming. He's seen voting's power ("wrenching" he says, to have waged a political campaign and not be able to vote). Now, he's using every tool possible to ensure what he wants gets accomplished.

many people stay home when it comes to local elections. This doesn't make sense, for the politicians elected and the measures approved or denied in local elections concern issues that are the closest to home. And where the electorate is smaller, the power and strength of individual voices increases radically.

## Voter Eligibility and Registration

When you reach voting age, do you just show up at the polls? Not that easy. In most states, voter registration is required since so many people vote. Have you ever signed up for a class or activity, and found when you first arrived, that your name was checked off during roll call? That's a registration process. Voter registration lets the registrar of voters know that you exist and enables voter information to be sent to you. The registration form asks about you, usually lists your state's eligibility requirements, and tells you by what date you need to register in order to be able to vote. You will need proof of residency and that you will be eighteen years of age or over by election day. A state has the right to deny the vote to residents of another state, those adjudged mentally incapacitated or convicted felons.

Now the bad news. The United States is low on the list of nations for ease of registration. Citizens actually must go out and find a registration form (not always that simple), fill it out, and return it. In some countries people actually go door to door to register citizens. In others, voting is compulsory! Here, you've got to make the effort.

*Compulsory voting has been an integral part of Australia's democracy since 1924. It ensures a high and therefore representative turnout at elections. It makes sure everyone has a stake in the result. In Australia voting is considered an obligation of citizenship just like paying taxes or abiding by the law. These obligations of citizenship, including compulsory voting, are what promotes our social and political cohesion. We have always believed that voting in Australia is a communal act by all Australians, an affirmation of their commitment to democracy and its public processes. Compulsory voting is the hallmark of our democratic electoral system.*

**John Faulkner**[5]
SENATOR FOR NSW, AUSTRALIA AND SHADOW MINISTER FOR
PUBLIC ADMINISTRATION AND GOVERNMENT SERVICES
THE CONSTITUTIONAL CONVENTION AND THE FIGHT AGAINST VOLUNTARY V

The National Voter Registration Act of 1993, nicknamed the "Motor Voter Act" made voter registration forms available at places we need to visit like the Department of Motor Vehicles, offices for public-assistance programs (AFDC, food stamps, Medicaid, etc.) and at Armed Forces recruitment centers. The federal Mail-in Voter Registration Application is now available on the Internet. In New York City, the Board of Elections arranged with the city's higher education system for voter registration mailers to be included in course registration packets.[6]

Our voter registration process is not the best, but it's becoming more available and simplified. Once registered, people are more likely to vote. While you're finding your voice, help other people find theirs by getting as many registered as possible.

## Political Parties

Political parties are formal groups of individuals who have joined together to promote political ideas they share through the electoral process. As a group, they can turn a rumble into a potent roar as the party swells with members. Today, the United States has two main political parties: the Democratic Party and Republican Party.

Democrats believe federal government's role is to protect citizens through national programs and act as a buffer against localized interests. A Democrat would prefer that general decisions over the standards of education be uniform throughout the states. Republicans feel that local and state governments are more attuned to the social and economic interests of the people they represent. If your state is a ranching state, Republicans might believe that state government regulates land use better than can the federal government whose administrators may have little knowledge of ranching.[7]

There are other political parties ("third parties"), some quite old and some newly created. Third parties have the advantage of a narrower focus and not having to be accountable to so many diverse interests. They can be more radical in their approach. Third party voters send a message that, even if slightly successful, will force others to take notice that something is going on they need to hear.[8] If the message is strong, it can grow into a major voice. The Republican Party was not formed until the

### Finding Out Voter and Registration Information

1. **Let your fingers do the walking:** In the government section of your local phone book under "voting," "voting registration," or "elections" find voter information from your County Board of Elections, County Registrar-Recorder or Secretary of State.

2. **Local offices of the political parties** will have voter information.

3. **On the Internet,** use keywords like "voter registration," "voting," "ballot," or "elections," and your state name.

4. **The Federal Voting Assistance Program (FVAP)** or voting officers on military bases, at embassies and consulates provide members (including family members) of the armed services or civilians working for the government abroad, with registration forms and ballots concerning voting issues and election dates for the specific state of residence.

1850s. For two decades prior, the Whig Party, along with the Democrats (formerly known as the Democratic-Republican Party, or Jeffersonians), dominated politics, but the Whigs split with in-fighting, too diverse membership and the failure to agree on the slavery issue.[9]

*Thomas Nast (1840–1902), a renowned Nineteenth Century political cartoonist, is credited with creating the donkey and elephant symbols of the Democratic and Republican Parties, respectively. The Democrats adopted the donkey as a symbol of homely, down-to-earth appeal. The Republicans felt the elephant denoted intelligence and impressive strength. Here are two of Thomas Nast's cartoons that inspired the adoption of these symbols.*

"A LIVE JACKASS KICKING A DEAD LION."

"THE THIRD-TERM PANIC."

## A Sampling of Contemporary Third Parties:[10]

(MANY OF THESE HAVE LINKS ON THE INTERNET AND CAN BE EXPLORED THERE.)

| | |
|---|---|
| Alaskan Independence Party | New Party |
| American Conservative Party | Patriot Party |
| American Tradition Party | Peace and Freedom Party |
| Communist Party USA | Peoples Revolutionary Party |
| Constitution Party of North Carolina | Progressive Labor Party |
| Green Party | Reform Party |
| Independence Party | Social Labor Party |
| League of Revolutionaries for a New America | Socialist Party USA |
| Libertarian Party | Socialist Workers Party |
| National Party | U.S. Taxpayers Party |
| Natural Law Party | Workers World Party |

IN EACH ELECTION, NEW THIRD PARTIES MAY FORM WHILE OTHERS GROW OR DECLINE IN POWER.

Knowledge of political parties is crucial so you can make proper choices when you vote since the candidates you vote for often carry the political baggage of their party. Joining a party can also quantify your chances of getting something done. Just investigate every candidate and policy, as well as the party, to see if your concerns are being met. What concerns most people transcends political parties. It is up to you to determine who, and which party, might work best for you and those you help to vote.

If others aren't saying what you want, but you still want to be heard, Independent is the way to go. You needn't be in a party to vote but you can miss the opportunity to vote in a primary, the election to decide which party candidate will run for a particular office. However, if your state has a "blanket" primary system, all voters can select from any of the candidates running for office.

What's so great about our system is that even if you join a political party, you don't need to fall in with the "party line"—all the candidates and issues backed by that party. We can vote freely and we vote along party lines only when we feel the need. Thus, on a general election ballot (or in an open primary) you could vote for a Republican, for a Democrat, or even for Beck or Will Smith in those states that allow you to write in anyone on the ballot, or for any registered write-in candidate in others.

> *There is no Democratic or Republican way of cleaning the streets.*
>
> **Fiorello La Guardia (1882–1947)**
> MAYOR OF NEW YORK CITY, 1933–1945

## Where and How to Vote

You've registered and/or convinced your parents and friends to register. Now, it's time to vote. The polling place's location is usually assigned by where you live. It can be in a public facility (schools, park buildings, county offices), a neighbor's house, the local motorcycle dealership, a beauty salon, a shopping mall, a church, or even on the beach. On election day the polls are usually open from 7 a.m. until 8 p.m. (check your local hours), and an American flag is hung outside. To record your presence and to ensure that you don't vote more than once, your name is checked off the list of registered voters and you are given a ballot, by party in primary elections, and directed to a voting booth.

"Hey! There's no soap in here."

The way that we vote is evolving as we speak as our school and working responsibilities, locations and hours have been changing dramatically. The inflexibility of the old voting standards—one set day, set hours, and old-fashioned voting methods —made the polls unavailable to many. State and federal election boards have heard voters say they feel disenfranchised when their lives and civic responsibilities cannot connect. The boards are using new methods, times, and places to vote to make it as convenient as possible for you to make your voice heard. Among current explorations are[11] :

**Electronic Voting Machines.** Newer electronic and/or computerized systems allow for flexibility in the poll's location, prevent mistakes and fraud with more secure

A New Type of Suffrage:

## OUTER SPACE VOTERS!

For the November 1997 elections, a Harris County, Texas ballot was sent by the county Chief of Elections to U.S. flight controllers in Moscow. The ballot was for **David Wolf**, a Harris County resident then aboard the Russian space station Mir. The controllers, using NASA's very sophisticated e-mail system, transmitted it to astronaut Wolf via his laptop computer. Wolf made his voting choices and e-mailed it back to Harris County via Moscow. The chief of elections opened the e-mail and manually punched a ballot with Wolf's choices.[13] One vote, one voice, all the way from outer space.

vote tallies, and act as demonstration machines for schools and the voting public. They can quickly sort and tally ballots by vote and party affiliation, and "lock out" ballot issues of no concern to a voter from one district while making them available to another.

**Internet Voting.**[12] For 2000's federal elections, the FVAP is putting five states' ballots on the Internet for those states' registered voters who are away from their traditional polling places in the military or civilian service abroad. This could be the first time that the Internet is used for a federal vote. If it works, election boards throughout the country will follow suit. You may be one of the first to vote via the Web!

**The Mail-in Ballot and Early Voting**. If you can't make the polls on election day, you can vote by mail or in person before the election in many states. By mail, you can obtain an absentee or mail-in ballot which contains the same candidates and propositions as the regular ballot. In some states you can vote in person before the actual election at sites as unusual as shopping malls and movie theaters. The early voting system opens satellite voting sites within the voting district for a specific number of days and expanded hours prior to the election. The location and number of sites (often mobile) are determined by factors such as population and geographic accessibility. In early voting, as with mail-in ballots, the results are not released until polls are closed on the formal election day so that others will not be influenced by these early votes.

Whatever the system your election board uses, learn it so that you understand the process. And if it's not comprehensive enough, think about change. Should we be able to vote at our schools, factories, or offices? On weekends? Next election, join your parents at the polls. See how the process really works. Check out the demonstration machines, and, when you can, vote!

### The Ballot

The actual ballot is less than awesome. No music. No graphics. Just the issues and candidates to vote on. A quiet way to exercise your big voice. It gets the job done.

First comes the sample ballot, sent to your registered address and sometimes available on the Internet. It names your polling place and lists the candidates for office and ballot propositions. In some states, the sample ballot includes text and summaries of each proposition, impact analyses, arguments and rebuttals, and candidate qualifications.

The Good News: Since the 1960s, elections take into account our increasingly multicultural nation. When the most current census shows a large citizen population using another language (according to a federally set formula), registration and ballots must be available in that language as well. Thus in a diverse area such as California's

Los Angeles County, election materials are currently available to voters in seven languages: English, Spanish, Japanese, Chinese, Vietnamese, Korean, and Tagalog.

The Bad News: In any language, the ballot can be hard to sort out but if you've done your homework, you'll know the candidates and issues and get through it.

In accordance with your state and district, you actually vote by pulling a lever, filling in bubbles, connecting arrows, punching holes in the ballot, marking an X by your choices, touching the surface of a screen, or using a computer if voting via the Internet.

However you do it, your vote counts. You can take your time, as did one recent voter who took forty-five minutes to vote.[14] To be fair to yourself and others, however, learn your district's election methods and prepare before you vote. Then take a list of your decisions with you to the polls. Complete your voting and that's it! Unless you can encourage others to vote before the polls close, just chill, and wait for the results.

## Counting the Ballots—Election Results

When the polls close, ballots are delivered, or totals reported, to a central location where they are counted for the precinct or district. Those vote totals, added to totals from all around the town, city, state, or country, absentee and early voting tallies, determine the success or failure of candidates and propositions. On election night or the next day, you'll find the course voters have set. Remember that politics are cyclical. If you don't agree with the results, you can work toward change in the next election.

## Presidential Elections and the Electoral College

The procedure for electing the president runs much like other elections with several distinct differences. Although anyone can place himself or herself on the ballot for office, we'll look at the major party candidate procedure for a tour of the system.

A candidate for president seeks his or her party's nomination. A campaign committee is formed. Fundraising begins and the candidate campaigns in state primaries or caucuses (local or district party meetings, often followed by state party conventions), appearing on as many primary ballots as thought to be useful. A state party may also run a "favorite son," a candidate they know will not win the presidency, but will have the ability to negotiate and transfer expected votes in the state's best interest.

This activity culminates at the national presidential nominating convention which takes place in the summer at a gathering of party members (delegates) from all over the country as well as prospective candidates. You've probably seen this on TV: Hordes moshing in a large hall, dodging signs with enough red, white, and blue on to make you think George Washington's been resurrected. Can you believe full-grown people—maybe some of your parents—are wearing "Miss America" sashes and funny straw hats ?

Who are these people??? They are registered voters and state residents who, in accordance with their state and their registered party's national committee rules, have indicated their interest in being considered as state delegates supporting a particular candidate. They are usually active party participants or strong supporters of a candidate. The method of selection varies widely between the Democratic and the Republican parties and from state to state.

Characteristically, Republicans give wide powers to their state parties in determining how and when delegates are selected. The Republican National Committee (RNC) sets the number of each state's delegates: three delegates and three alternates per congressional district.[15] The RNC also sets the time period in which delegates are to be selected—at present from February to mid-June of the election year.

The Democratic National Committee (DNC) sets its rules from the "top up".[16] Within the first six months of a presidential election year, states select "district-level" and "at-large" delegates who pledge their votes to their candidate of choice, and "superdelegates": DNC members, certain federal and state elected officials, former presidents, vice-presidents, leaders of the Senate, speakers of the House and current House members.[17] The delegation's size is determined by an equation of population, federal districting and the Democratic presidential and major election voting record.

Republican or Democrat, delegate selection is affected by whether the state selects presidential candidates by primary election—where voters cast their ballots for their presidential preference and rank-and-file delegates are then proportionally allocated —or a caucus convention. In the caucus system, delegates run in local party meetings, which lead to large district meetings and ultimately to a state convention where a final vote is taken to determine which candidate's state delegates go to the national convention. Once delegates are selected, their names are sent to the national party and entered into the temporary rolls of the party as they prepare for the convention.

At the national conventions (in the summer before the November election), roll calls of the delegates are taken. A presidential candidate is nominated to run against the other party's candidate. The party platform explaining the political goals for the election is created and approved and a vice-presidential candidate is chosen. The presidential nominee, consulting political advisors and experienced party leaders, chooses his or her running mate. Often, the vice presidential candidate will be someone representing other views within the party in an effort to attract as many voters as possible. Another delegate roll call confirms that choice. When you vote for president, you vote a "ticket" (president and vice president). This is not necessarily true in other races. For example, governors and the lieutenant governors may be of different political parties.

One confusing note—remember that the Founding Fathers limited who could vote at the country's creation? Most exclusions are gone, but one lingers and drives students, their teachers, and most adults to distraction during presidential election years. For the Founders just didn't trust the common man when it came to voting, especially for president. They also didn't want to give Congress primary power to choose the top executive. So, with the weight of responsibility on them, the Founders established an unusual system to ostensibly protect the office of the president: the Electoral College. [18]

When you vote, you are making what is called a popular vote but the popular vote does not directly elect the president. In most states it only determines which presidential candidate carries that state. For example, if the popular vote (plurality) in your state favors the Democratic candidate, the electors elected by the state Democratic Party spring into action. The Republican electors nominated by the state Republican party disappear, except in those few states where electors are picked by other methods, including proportionment by congressional district.

The number of each state's electors is determined by the number of its members of Congress (the number of representatives plus the two senators). In total, 538 electoral votes are available to elect a president, based on the total number of senators in the Senate (100) and representatives in the House of Representatives (435) plus three additional electors from the District of Columbia. A majority vote (more than 270 electoral votes) is required to select the president and vice-president, each selected separately. If not, the members of the House of Representatives select by majority vote.

In mid-December, electors convene in their state capital and vote supposedly for the candidate of their party. The tally is delivered to the current vice president of the United States, who acts as president of the Senate, and to the Speaker of the House for tabulation jointly by House and Senate in early January. The vice president, as presiding officer of this joint session of Congress, then announces the winner.

According to the Constitution, electors really don't have to vote for their party's candidate but can vote any way they like. However, condemnation for a "faithless elector" in states requiring electors to cast their votes according to the

The President of the United States of necessity owes his election to office to the suffrage and zealous labors of a political party, the members of which cherish with ardor and regard as of essential importance the principles of their party organization; but he should strive to be always mindful of the fact that he serves his party best who serves the country best.

**Rutherford B. Hayes** (1822–1893)
PRESIDENT OF THE UNITED STATES
(1877–1881)
INAUGURAL ADDRESS, MARCH 5, 1877

# Electoral College

## Total: 538    Majority Needed to Elect: 270

| | | |
|---|---|---|
| ALABAMA – 9 | LOUISIANA – 9 | OKLAHOMA – 8 |
| ALASKA – 3 | MAINE – 4 | OREGON – 7 |
| ARIZONA – 8 | MARYLAND – 10 | PENNSYLVANIA – 23 |
| ARKANSAS – 6 | MASSACHUSETTS – 12 | RHODE ISLAND – 4 |
| CALIFORNIA – 54 | MICHIGAN – 18 | SOUTH CAROLINA – 8 |
| COLORADO – 8 | MINNESOTA – 10 | SOUTH DAKOTA – 3 |
| CONNECTICUT – 8 | MISSISSIPPI – 7 | TENNESSEE – 11 |
| DELAWARE – 3 | MISSOURI – 11 | TEXAS – 32 |
| DISTRICT OF COLUMBIA – 3 | MONTANA – 3 | UTAH – 5 |
| FLORIDA – 25 | NEBRASKA – 5 | VERMONT – 3 |
| GEORGIA – 13 | NEVADA – 4 | VIRGINIA – 13 |
| HAWAII – 4 | NEW HAMPSHIRE – 4 | WASHINGTON – 11 |
| IDAHO – 4 | NEW JERSEY – 15 | WEST VIRGINIA – 5 |
| ILLINOIS – 22 | NEW MEXICO – 5 | WISCONSIN – 11 |
| INDIANA – 12 | NEW YORK – 33 | WYOMING – 3 |
| IOWA – 7 | NORTH CAROLINA – 14 | |
| KANSAS – 6 | NORTH DAKOTA – 3 | |
| KENTUCKY – 8 | OHIO – 21 | |

popular vote can include fines, disqualification and, most assuredly, not being nominated again!

It generally works like this: If the Republican candidate A gains 2,750,000 votes in Ohio and Democratic candidate B has 1,800,000 votes, all of Ohio's electoral votes go to A. But, even if A wins the popular vote in the country, if B wins more states with a greater number of electoral votes, candidate B wins. Supposedly this system protects the interests of the smaller states whose popular vote might be low based upon population. At least they say so.

Notwithstanding all this, your vote still counts. By making it, you added to the popular vote, thus determining which electors vote for the president. So just vote. Presidential elections are the toughest, but they usually work out. In all cases but the 1824, 1876, and 1888 elections, the electoral vote has followed the popular vote. And remember, whatever you think about the electoral college system and whether it works for the country or not, there are two other important branches of national government: the Congress and the Judiciary. Congressional members are elected by direct vote and the Judiciary appointed by those you elect. Your vote and voice will always have an effect.

# Has a President Ever Been Elected When the Popular Vote Went for Another Candidate?

In 1824, **Andrew Jackson** won the popular vote but failed to achieve a majority of electoral votes. Neither did the other three candidates. The House of Representatives decided. There, thirteen state delegations (a majority then) voted for John Quincy Adams, who won neither the popular vote nor the electoral vote, but thus became president.

In 1876, although **Rutherford B. Hayes** (R) lost the popular vote, questions were raised about four states' electoral votes. An electoral commission established by Congress decided in favor of the Republican votes and Hayes became the president.

In 1888, although **Grover Cleveland** won the popular vote, the majority of electoral votes went to **Benjamin Harrison**, who became president.

When the popular vote was overturned in the 1800s, news did not travel fast and, in most cases, the electors were listed along with the presidential candidates on the ballot. Today, electors are not listed and many have forgotten that the electoral vote determines our presidential outcome. Imagine the public dismay and confusion if our popular presidential choice was announced by our "fast-breaking" news on election night, but then overturned two months later in January![20]

KGB "97"

# Writing Your Own Tales, Helena, Montana[21]

High noon in the real West. Strolling down the street is someone with a shaved head, ready for a showdown. Clint Eastwood directing. Whoa! Wrong book! Or is it?

**Molly Madden**, sixteen, of Helena, Montana, is readying for the OK Corral, but on her terms and on her own issues. The enemy here: the subtle forms of bigotry we all can succumb to.

A shaved-headed young woman in a state often known for shaved heads and militaristic leanings shouldn't be an oddity. But Molly Madden is—an independent high school junior who shaves her head twice weekly to combat stereotypes of any sort, including the usual assumptions about "skinheads" and a woman's appearance.

Molly has founded a human rights group for teens called Youth for Unity. It is a group purposely without structure and run by "kids" (whom Molly defines as middle school, high school, kids who have graduated—"anyone who thinks they are still a kid"). Molly understands that how information is presented greatly affects how it's processed and how decisions are made and feels an adult sponsor might taint the information her group wants. She says, "We didn't want to have administrators or sponsors who would worry if we stepped on anyone's toes. We want to be on top of people's toes,"

Youth for Unity wants to help everyone to live together. They meet regularly, talk and argue about issues, and decide, individually, what they need to do to help their community and themselves. They debate the truth of information brought into the meetings and assumptions made by others regarding what they hear and see.

So who comes to the meetings? The expected—the school leaders, student council members, the soccer players, the usual activists. But who else? Those with green hair and chains. Those the first group probably hadn't even noticed were at the same school.

That's the point for Molly. This isn't school, nor is it a one-issue, one-direction organization. And the kids are coming. From six the first time, to the six plus six of their friends the second, and on from there—the equivalent of a Montana stampede. They are networking, learning about each other, and how their collective effort can change lives.

· What's been Youth for Unity's effect? Instead of hanging around being bored and getting into trouble, a restaurant in Helena is becoming the weekly place to be. Those who felt alienated from the system are creating systems of their own, making their own decisions. It's been rather cool.

Youth for Unity is tackling amazing projects from concerts benefiting community or national issues to helping other organizations recruit teen support. They want to make things happen. Some current concerns: intolerance in all forms, sweatshops and child labor, the neo-Nazi movement, women's issues, and gay rights. They take no sides as a group and work to create advocacy opportunities for what members believe. With a small-scale group and city they understand their power is in bringing issues out in the open for discussion and change. And change fans out, as more teens in Helena and neighboring towns hear about what Youth for Unity is accomplishing.

Molly uses a three-step process: awareness, decision-making, and activism. Awareness: find out about issues, how they affect you, and what you can do. Decision-making: decide whether "to sit around and whine" or whether to attend meetings, get information, and plan an action. Activism: ensure that what is intended is actually done.

Helena's community is benefiting from this building chorus. Youth for Unity has proposed a sensitivity and diversity training program for the school curriculum. A "Diversity Week" for her high school designed by Molly is modeled upon assemblies and sports week programs. It will introduce ideas and speakers not always as available to students in such a homogeneous state including skinheads, Holocaust survivors, Native Americans, and representatives of other political, racial, and social groups. Kids will be encouraged to support alternative lifestyles and cultural heritage issues by dressing and acting symbolically (for example, wearing purple if they support diversity).

Molly is going about this project carefully because she understands that kids want to see effective and immediate results of their efforts, a lesson learned through her own experience. Under the sponsorship of a leadership conference, Molly wrote the President asking if kids were to attend his White House Conference on Hate Crimes and, on the premise that "youth are the best teachers of other youth," could she participate? To strengthen her request, Molly called in political "chips" (favors), seeking political and financial support from Helena's mayor, one of Montana's senators and Montana's human rights network, among others. A personal letter from the president confirmed her attendance. And so she went. An important meeting, but not well represented by young people and while well intentioned, in Molly's view, the solutions proposed were too complex for immediate results.

From this experience, Molly knows that when a conference is planned, it must focus on being productive, an advantage of the smaller local pond in which Youth for Unity works. Diversity Week is the first. On tap: a Labor Day conference on identity, providing networking opportunities for youth and aid with the important "who's" of their life right now: who they are, who they aren't, and who they want to be. Next: conferences and concerts about objectivity in thought and action, establishing several subchapters in other areas of Montana, and carrying on her three-step process.

With this model of clear and pragmatic thinking, Molly and Youth for Unity are taking ownership of their ideas and redefining the duel between doing nothing and doing a lot. With the political power emanating from this posse of youth, intolerance can be disarmed before sundown, and we'll all still be there when dawn arrives.

*"When I use a word," Humpty Dumpty said, in a rather scornful tone, "it means just what I choose it to mean—neither more nor less."*

*"The question is," said Alice, "whether you can make words mean so many different things."*

*"The question is," said Humpty Dumpty, "which is to be master—that's all."*

**Lewis Carroll (Charles L. Dodgson) (1832–1898)**
**THROUGH THE LOOKING-GLASS (AND WHAT ALICE FOUND THERE), 1872**

# Knowledge is Power

Democracy. Voting. Using our voice. So much of what we do is based on having information with which to support our beliefs. If we want to make a change, how do we know what needs to be changed? If someone asks us to do something, how do we know it's right for us? If we're faced with two people who want to lead us, how do we choose? Will they hear us? Will we hear them? Democracy gives us the right to ask both "Why?" and "Why not?"

This chapter is about questioning. It is about gathering information and turning it into knowledge by running it through our own experience to give us the vocabulary of effective voice. It makes others listen and it gets things done. Knowledge is power.

Information is everywhere and in many disguises. It comes cloaked in headlines, ads, and cartoons in the morning paper, magazines, and comic books you read. It's in the news between songs on your favorite radio station and in the songs themselves. It's on TV through the news, the docudramas, talk shows, sitcoms, and infomercials. It filters through the movies and weaves into conversations with parents, teachers, friends, pastors, and counselors. It lounges on the walls of the buildings in your community as posters, graffiti, and billboards. Information can be fact. It can be opinion. It can be propaganda. What you do with the information is up to you.

Stay with your favorite FM station during its five-minute newsbreak. Even five minutes can keep you current on what's going on in the world. Read the morning newspaper. Even if you just read film or music news, you're learning how others see society, expressed through the entertainment produced for you to consume.

When you're glued to the TV, don't start surfing the channels at news time. You like their music and programming. You might like their take on the day's events. (And don't forget about CNN, CNBC, BET, A&E, PBS, ESPN, TBS, the networks, and even MTV, among others.)

If you're hacking around in cyberspace, sign on to teen chat rooms to see if others think like you about an issue, candidate, or program. You can download news and hang out in a variety of interesting newsgroups. They don't know you're a teen and you'll see if "adult" conversation is really all it's cracked up to be. You can also find specific political rooms and other fact/discussion newsgroups that might interest you.

> *Some men see things as they are and say "why?" I dream things that never were and say, "why not?"*
>
> **John Fitzgerald Kennedy (1917–1963)**[1]
> PRESIDENT OF THE UNITED STATES, 1960–1963

> *If a Nation expects to be ignorant and free in a state of civilization, it expects what never was and never will be. . . If we are to guard against ignorance and remain free, it is the responsibility of every American to be informed.*
>
> **Thomas Jefferson (1743–1826)**
> PRESIDENT OF THE UNITED STATES, 1801–1809

## Kids AND *Adults:* How Do We Learn?

We learn from our own personal experience and that of others. We learn from reality—a fact so uncontested that we all have to agree to its truth. We learn how to think, not what to think. We do this by reading, watching, listening, experiencing, and questioning.

We investigate our questions.
We ask our parents.
We ask our teachers.
We ask our friends.
We ask children.
We use our own eyes, ears, and brain and ask ourselves.
We use our library and research sources.
We use our media.
We try out our thoughts.
We ask again.
We discuss.

# Lauren Gaffney[2]
## *A Play without Ending in Many Acts*, **Summit, New Jersey**

**ACT I:**

**SCENE 1:** Lauren Gaffney's vocal coach dies of AIDS when Lauren is eleven. His gift to her: a dramatic lesson in commitment—to her talent and to her world, a casting call to the drama of HIV/AIDS, which gnaws away not only at the creative community, but the everyday world of kids infected through childbirth or unsafe sex.

**SCENE 2:** Lauren, now thirteen, is set to open in a new Broadway musical. As a gift to the other cast members (a theater tradition), she creates a new AIDS awareness ribbon, slightly altering the traditional red looped ribbon by forming a heart into the upper loop to symbolize "the love and caring young people have for children with AIDS."

**SCENE 3:** Typical showbiz. The show doesn't open. However, the rehearsals were not in vain. Dispelling the myth that kids don't get involved, Lauren reaffirms her faith in her own generation, calling on them to join the fight against AIDS. Her goal: increase teen awareness, knowledge, and responsibility toward the epidemic.

**ACT II:**

**SCENE 1:** Using her theater contacts, Lauren contacts Broadway Cares/Equity Fights AIDS (BC/EFA), the powerful group behind theater's aggressive stance against the disease. With BC/EFA, Lauren organizes community outreach events in the tri-state area, culminating in an inaugural event for Lauren's new nonprofit organization, Kids Can! (Kids Care AIDS Network)—a major benefit concert in New York City, involving performances of over 100 young professional actors, dancers, and singers.

**SCENE 2:** Kids and the theater network sell tickets that net an astounding $28,000, distributed to several pediatric AIDS centers and ensure the network's startup.

**ACT III:**

Phone calls. Papers flying. Kids Can! is born. Its mission: "to unite young people in schools and communities nationwide to participate in the fight against HIV/AIDS." An information and resource center on

*If everyone is thinking alike then somebody isn't thinking.*

**General George S. Patton (1885–1945)**
**U.S. GENERAL, WORLD WAR II**

If your first venture raises questions, think about how you can go further. If you started with a newspaper headline, read the rest of the article. Follow it for several days. It may be moved inside as the news gets "old." Look farther back in the paper. Real news is often hidden. In large cities, you may have to hunt for local news. But local news, like local elections, is about what you, your family, and your friends deal with every day. If you heard something on MTV, check it out in the paper, on the Net, or the Web, it describes the disease and how to prevent it and helps those already infected. Kids send Kids Can! their AIDS projects for showcasing on the web site. The Network creates and sponsors fund-raising projects to assist children and families living with HIV/AIDS.

ACT IV:

**SCENE 1:** Lauren's friends rally to make ribbons (sold for 50 cents on her website and through BC/EFA), while the website instructs others who make and sell them to raise funds for pediatric AIDS.

**SCENE 2:** Now a symbol of kids' efforts against HIV/AIDS, Lauren's ribbon is starring on BC/EFA's holiday greeting card and on T-shirts sold to raise money. It's out on road tour on lapels and clothing everywhere.

ACT V:

**SCENE 1:** Using their talents to join the battle, young performers stage a benefit reading of a play about young people dealing with AIDS. Lauren uses her stage skills to speak at conventions and leadership conferences about pediatric AIDS.

**SCENE 2:** Lauren meets with political leaders, civic organizations such as the Points of Light Foundation, New Jersey's governor, and Congressional representatives to bring the power of teen concern to those able to legislate and inspire programs.

ENCORE:

Still starring in this drama, Lauren voted for the first time one week after she turned eighteen, ready to ensure that local, state, and federal government will not be let off the hook until the disease is understood (money for education), the infected are supported (money for health care), and the cure is found (money for research).

with your parents, teachers, and friends. See if there's more to it. See if there's another side.

Read the paper's editorials and letters to the editor. They openly represent points of view—the paper's and the public's respectively. They are of interest because they present opinions of what the facts mean. So long as you know where they are coming from, you can use these opinions in making your own decision about an issue.

People with an agenda know there is power in numbers and they will want you to join with them. You may choose to do so if you know that their interests are close to your concerns. However, although they may stand for a cause you like, how can you make sure you like whatever else they're doing?

If a candidate says something that interests you–research it before you react. Be wary of buzzwords the candidate may use to appeal to your emotions. Ask others what they think. Look into candidate's records (past votes, business or professional practice). Read about public officials in newspapers and magazines. Contact the candidate's campaign office for more information. Check out the US Government Printing Office and the Internet for pamphlets on important issues and where this candidate stands on them.

Once you've got the information, go one step further and sift through all those little infobits in search of the truth.

## Fact, Opinion, and Propaganda:

**Fact:** something that exists or has actually happened that can be proven by reason or evidence. It's a fact that you're processing these words, that the sun sets in the evening. It's a fact that Carlos went surfing if you watched him catch that humungous wave yesterday. But if you only saw Carlos at the local fast food spot with his surfboard on top of his car, you cannot state as a fact that he had been surfing that day without other concrete evidence. If you knew his surfing habits, logic might tell you what Carlos had been doing, but you're not necessarily stating a fact. He could have been too lazy to take the board off the car the night before.

**Opinion**: a belief that is not based on absolute certainty or positive knowledge, but seems to be true although it cannot be absolutely proven. Opinions are most of what we hear: "I think that . . . ," "I believe that . . . ," "It may be that . . . ," even sometimes "I know that . . . ." If Maneka says, "I'm sure Carlos was surfing because he usually surfs after school," she's registering an opinion as to his activity based upon Carlos's usual behavior. But it still isn't a fact, because she really didn't see him surf.

**Propaganda:** a deliberate effort to persuade people to support or adopt a particular idea. Sounds harmless enough. It's not.

So much of what we read or hear today falls within the propaganda category. The words entice us. Remember how, when you were small, you had to have the "newest," "coolest" thing you saw on TV that "all kids have"? Was it always what you expected?

Propaganda takes opinions and points of view and passes them off as facts. It often uses information incorrectly. It uses rumors. Propaganda is advertising. It wants to sell us a product or concept: the newest jeans, CD, tickets, fast food. It wants to sell us a political point of view. The language of propaganda sets things up as truth: "The greatest. . .," "Everyone is. . .," "The only. . .," "The best. . . ."

*"Slogans can be worse than swords if they are only put in the right mouths."*

**Zora Neale Hurston (1891–1960)**
AMERICAN NOVELIST, FOLKLORIST, AND
ANTHROPOLOGIST
MOSES, MAN OF THE MOUNTAIN, (1939)

It's okay to want to agree with our friends–to want to belong. Sometimes we'll accept propaganda when it isn't that important. Sometimes it encourages us to do something we might not otherwise do–like trying out a new food that we weren't so sure of and loving it, or listening to a band we've never heard of before. What's not okay is when someone with an agenda so different from ours tries to take us in by using words that persuade us they think the same way we do. That's a problem.

Propaganda messes with our heads. It tells us what to do and what to think. It doesn't want us to ask questions and that's dangerous. There's

## Who's Telling Me What to Do?

First your parents, then your teachers and then your friends, plus this short list:

★ older brothers and sisters and other family members
★ peer/social groups
★ television—dramas, sitcoms, cartoons, "reality" shows, VJs, newscasters, actors, talk-show hosts, infomercials, commercials
★ music and radio— CDs and recording artists, DJs, newscasters, talk-radio hosts, and commercials
★ newspapers, tabloids, and magazines—owners, publishers, editors, reporters, and advertisers
★ books—publishers, authors, and editors
★ films—writers, producers, actors, marketers, studio executives
★ theater—playwrights, actors, producers
★ videos—dramas, actors, producers, directors, commercials
★ celebrities, including those from the worlds of sports and media fame
★ toy, book, computer, video, and clothing companies who pay for advertising on the TV, news, magazines, and radio you watch and listen to
★ marketing analysts who determine what you will read, watch, and listen to in order to buy their clients' products
★ pollsters—whose polls fit their purpose and convince you to be part of a group
★ employers
★ other adults in charge
★ government—administrators, legislators, and enforcers
★ this book

nothing wrong in agreeing with suggestions people make, just make sure it's after you have enough information.[3]

## Bias

To explain bias, let's start with your best standard: you. How do you take in information? Can you filter it through your good sense and experience and tell when it's fact, opinion, or propaganda and use it accordingly? A preconceived opinion or inclination can get in the way of how you might interpret something and lead you to conclusions that are prejudicial and stereotyped. That is your bias. All of us have to be careful not to fall into the bias trap. It is far easier to generalize than find out the truth.

Modern politics understands the persuasive value of media and polls—surveys taken of a small number of people on specific issues and then deemed representative of a whole group. In 30-second political commercials, set-format debates, and headlines there's not much time to discover the reasons for a candidate's or issue's position and the propaganda convinces us to believe and give our support.

Propaganda plays upon our biases and we may not even know it for bias is complex, involving many factors including race, religion, gender, age, ethnicity, culture, nationality, geographic location, and wealth. We are the product of many influences and it pays to understand how we perceive things before deciding how to act.

*Your bait of falsehood takes this carp of truth;*

*And thus do we of wisdom and of reach,*

*With windlasses and with assays of bias,*

*By indirections find directions out.*

**William Shakespeare (1564–1616)**
HAMLET, ACT II, SCENE L

Would an older candidate's age influence whether or not you give your support? Do you think that someone older is totally out of it? If you look at the history of politics and government, elderly participants are often the greatest leaders, using their years of experience to formulate effective legislation.

Conversely, why vote for anyone young? They aren't experienced enough to deal with the older politicians and won't be able to get anything done. Yet, while experience plays a role, so do passion and commitment. Today's youth are extremely knowledgeable and articulate and able to get things done.

How about this candidate? He has a lovely blond wife and two cute little daughters, lives in a lovely little home, and professes to be concerned with the family.

Hold on! The family values candidate could be a major real estate developer running for a local office that has control over your community's land development. Family notwithstanding, you may not want to support someone who may have a financial interest in the outcome of programs under his charge. The experienced elderly candidate's voting record may show he has consistently voted against spending money for new business in urban areas and your family is trying to put together a group to attract a new market to your neighborhood. The young candidate may be smart, but far too interested in moving up the political ladder to be concerned with homelessness and a resultant petty crime problem in his district.

Two additional examples: An African-American candidate seems the likely choice in a predominantly African-American area, and you want to see more African-Americans in office. But are you sure this candidate is the best for the job? Or, a candidate for another office is openly gay. You agree with her platform but don't support her lifestyle. However, her opponent is politically opposed to everything you believe in. Is sexual preference the issue here or is it getting what you want done?

Look at the qualifications of the opponent then again at the qualifications of your front-runner before you make that decision. Your bias may revolve around only one aspect of the candidate's whole. Question it before it limits you to only half the truth.

Asking yourself what you really feel, if you don't have to prove anything to

> The purpose of having seats where minority communities have a majority of the electorate is not so they can a priori elect a minority [candidate]. . . . Let the debate unfold and let democracy take its course. The playing field is level. Let the leaders make their opinions known, let the voters make their choice, and let the chips fall where they may.

**Antonio González**
PRESIDENT OF SOUTHWEST VOTER REGISTRATION EDUCATION PROJECT (COMMENTING UPON A JUNE 1995 RACE FOR A SEAT ON THE LOS ANGELES BOARD OF EDUCATION FROM A LARGELY LATINO DISTRICT BETWEEN TWO QUALIFIED CANDIDATES—ONE LATINO, ONE ANGLO.)[4]

## TeenVotes—
## Who Wants Them—and Why?[5]

**1998, BARROW, ALASKA.** The "local option law" has again come up for a vote.

Alaska, a state with major alcoholism problems in its rural communities and a fetal alcohol syndrome rate up to ten times the national average, allows communities to regulate the sale, possession, and consumption of alcohol through a number of different options, ranging from completely "wet" to "damp" (legal to possess and import, illegal to sell) to totally "dry" (no alcohol is allowed to be either possessed or sold in the community). Alaska's legal drinking age is twenty-one. The teens who can vote but can't drink are being courted by the damp/wet lobbies who are using the words "personal freedom" to lure them.

"Personal freedom" vs. "community well-being"—both well-respected phrases.

How would you decide?

anyone, will help you recognize when you go on automatic and give you control as you recognize who you are and then, what you can do about it. Here are some questions:

★Is this a generalization on my part or really related to the candidate or issue?
★Is my bias my own or am I simply repeating things my family or friends say?
★Am I hearing what people are saying, or am I changing the words to the way I want them to be?
★Am I basing my opinion on how a candidate looks or the campaign sounds?
★Do I think a candidate is great because he or she looks just like me?
★Am I listening and looking?

*To be nobody but yourself in a world which is doing its best, night and day, to make you everybody else means to fight the hardest battle which any human being can fight; and never stop fighting.*

**E.E. Cummings (1984–1962)**
**EXCERPT FROM "A POET'S ADVICE TO STUDENTS," A MISCELLANY REVISED**[6]

## Media Literacy

Media literacy is learning how to figure out the difference between fact, opinion, propaganda, and bias in what we watch, read, and hear.

Aside from the information we take in through our own perception and discussion with others, media is basically the vehicle through which information downloads to us. It includes advertising, movies, television, radio, music, video games, books, tabloids, comic books, magazines, "zines," newspapers, and websites.

Information is often the product of bias, influenced by the attitude and background of its creators or providers. We tend to take messages as fact, but unless we know the point of view under which the information is created and delivered, how will we know if we're being manipulated? We need to learn how to cut through the propaganda that is often disguised as "fact" or "news."

Newspapers, magazines, e-business, and radio and television stations make money by selling space and commercial airtime for product and service advertisements. Movies are sensational to draw greater numbers of ticket and popcorn buyers into the theaters and to increase video sales and rentals.

Competition pressures commercial media to present news and entertainment that captures a greater audience. This pressure can result in news, programs, and products that take a definitely biased view or that are sensationalized but we may not know it. As consumers, we must learn how to read, see, and hear again and to filter out the distortion. Otherwise, we might choose something that we never really wanted or reject something good for us. It's time to take media information apart, deconstruct it, and find its bias.

*It is the mark of an educated mind to be able to entertain a thought without accepting it.*

**Aristotle** (384–323 B.C.)
**PHILOSOPHER**

*Believe nothing . . . merely because you have been told it. . . .or because it is traditional, or because you yourselves have imagined it. Do not believe what your teacher tells you merely out of respect for the teacher. But whatsoever, after due examination and analysis, you find to be conducive to the good, the benefit, the welfare of all beings—that doctrine believe and cling to, and take it as your guide.*

**Attributed to Siddhartha Gautama [Buddha]** (c.563–483 B.C.)

One thing to remember: Bias is not necessarily bad. We don't want to get too cynical, as issues may be extremely complex. For example: A filmmaker concerned about global warming may create a documentary on the plight of animals in forests being cut down for timber. Another filmmaker concerned with economic issues may cover that same issue with a documentary on the severe economic problems faced by the people around the forest if they cannot earn money lumbering. Two different stories with opposing points of view. Both have truth. Find out who is making the argument while you take in the information and then figure out where you stand.

### HOW DO WE USE INFORMATION TO COMBAT AN OPINION AND BUILD AN ARGUMENT?

When your parents read a news item today with the large headline "Battle at the Concert" and a photograph from a rock or rap concert you're planning to attend tomorrow and the photo shows some evil-looking guys doing stuff evil guys might do, what do you think their reaction will be when you tell them you're going? They don't know that almost everyone else at the concert was okay and that it was a safe place to be. Without other photos or text, they only see the worst.

How can you change their minds?

**1. Get first-hand factual reports** that these were the only incredibly evil-looking guys there and most were just regular kids enjoying the sound.

**2. Find an item in another paper** or zine to back this up.

**3. Call the venue to ask how safe the concert was.**

With facts, your parents might be convinced that the reporter and photographer picked out the only semi-interesting event and built it up to headline proportions. If something matters to you, you can get beyond the bias and change people's minds.

Delivering news is storytelling after all. Often, when it is printed or aired on TV, things are left out and facts or opinions are emphasized to increase the drama and the sales. Most news is reported fairly, but it pays to be on the watch for bias.

## THE EVOLUTION OF MAN

 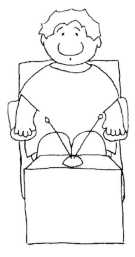

# Checking Out the News[7]

There may be more or less to a story than is reported and what is altered can make it a very different story and message. Is the headline true to the facts? Where is the story? On the front page (most important for sales), inside, or in back? At the top of the TV news or after the sports?

Is it there at all? Stories are suppressed sometimes for the most innocent of reasons (space) and sometimes deliberately. Placement is often less issue driven than to sell papers or get the remote control stuck on the channel.

A photo can influence your opinion depending upon the choice of subject, how it is shot, and where it is placed. The caption description can influence your reaction.

We are easily influenced by the tone of the news piece. Is it positive or negative? Are there any words or phrases designed to press your emotional buttons without giving you time to stop and think what is really being said? Classic examples often used: One man's "freedom fighter" is another's "terrorist." An "ex-con" can be someone who served for a minor offense twenty years ago and has been a great citizen since.

What was the source of the news? Who supplied the information? The on-site reporter, eyewitness, police, fire officials, executives, government officials, friends, family, or neighbors of the perpetrator or of the victim? Or was it supplied by press agents or campaign workers hired to promote celebrities, public persons, and politicians? Knowing the source, you can determine whether you are being given the whole story.

*Those of us who shout the loudest about Americanism in making character assassinations are all too frequently those who, by our own words and acts, ignore some of the basic principles of Americanism—The right to criticize. The right to hold unpopular beliefs. The right to protest. The right of independent thought.*

**Senator Margaret Chase Smith (R) (1897–1995)**
FIRST WOMAN ELECTED TO BOTH HOUSES OF CONGRESS AND FIRST WOMAN TO HAVE HER NAME PLACED IN NOMINATION FOR PRESIDENT BY A MAJOR POLITICAL PARTY.
REMARKS IN THE SENATE, JUNE 1, 1950, V. 96, P. 7894

Television requires even more attention, especially when we're faced with infomercials and paid political campaign advertisements. This is propaganda run rampant. Sprawled in front of the tube, we tend to stop questioning and it is harder for us to be critical. Yet the messages we receive in our slothlike state are the ones that burrow deep.

Kids are the easiest prey for propaganda. When you were younger, think about how often you wanted the products all those actors, superheroes, and music groups were promoting just because you thought the sellers were so cool. Now you are old enough to know that substantial money is paid to celebrities and role models for promotion. Some of the products are good and some are not, but that's irrelevant to the way they are sold. The ads play upon your emotions and your desires. People in commercials, including kids, are selected to look better and brighter than real people. So too are politicians.

# Take Apart **Political Spots**

Here are some **buzzwords** to watch out for:

★ **"American people"** and **"My fellow Americans"**: Does the candidate mean all citizens or only people like himself? White? Black? Christian? Asian? Hispanic? Militant? Conservative? Liberal?

★ **"Welfare cheats," "Deserving poor,"** and "**Welfare reform**": What agenda is the speaker pushing with these words. Whose interest is being represented?

★ **"Censorship"**: Is this call to arms being used appropriately or as a generic defense to any criticism of speech or action?

★ "**Budget reform**": Money is everyone's concern, young or old. But in politics, finance is filled with many complex issues and whenever someone proposes an easy solution ("tax cut," "tax revision," "balanced budgets"), there are many ways in which it may affect what you do, where you live and what your schools, communities, and jobs may have available for you.

★ **"Entitlements"**: To what are we really entitled?

★ **"Quotas"**: A classic: "One man's 'quotas' are another's 'affirmative action' ".

★ **"Liberal"** or **"Right-wing"**: Originally describing people with certain political philosophies, they have become negative epithets hurled by opponents.

★ **"Family values"**: While ostensibly something we would all support, the terms have been adopted by specific issue groups to promote their agendas.

How is the candidate being positioned? This is "celebrity time." **Image and personality** play major roles in campaigns. But who are we electing? We all like Donald Duck, but can he solve the problems of unemployment and education?

Look at the use of **color and the lighting, camera angle, and focus** to see how the choice can affect the way we view a person or a dramatic rendering of an issue.

What **music** is playing? Is it pleasing for agreement? Is it harsh when an opponent is mentioned? Is it your favorite tune of the moment or something that puts you in a nostalgic mood? Does the music say anything about the candidate or issue or does it align its emotion with what you might be asked to feel about what's being promoted?

**Who appears** in the spot? Actors? Real people? If real, who are they? Must you agree with them? Are they your family, friends, and neighbors? What is their bias?

How is the issue positioned? **Are our fears and our desires being played upon?** Are they based in the reality of what the passage or denial of this measure will do?

Ask the questions. You'll get to your answers.

"Do we need to represent anyone else in this commercial? We've already got a nurturing father with his baby, some active senior citizens, a little girl playing football, construction workers checking out books at a library, some very attractive women who weigh more than 150 pounds, deaf yuppies, . . ."

Let's take apart a political spot. It's not hard to figure out what the candidates and their handlers want you to see. Remember how quick a TV spot is. Almost everything a candidate says is in "sound bites"–a sentence or two packed with words and tones designed to make you say "yeah."

The length, presentation, and format of the spot can distort your understanding of what's being said. Are the proponents of a candidate or measure giving good reasons why you should support that candidate or issue? What is the issue? Is it stated accurately, or is something brought up to take the focus away from hard-hitting facts that might give you reason to question their viewpoint?

## Rating the Candidates

When you look at candidates, you can use all the above tools and get past bias. The winner of the election is going to be your voice. Find out what is important in each candidate's character–what it will mean for the office sought and promises made–and compare that with what is important to you. The candidate could look like the Loch Ness monster, and you will not care if the goals are just like yours whereas political ties to others, especially those whose policies you don't like, can be very important.

Be aware that, as human beings, our politicians may change as they mature in their political life, and not always the way we want them to grow. Sometimes young liberal Democrats become more conservative. Sometimes Republicans become Democrats. Sometimes issues once important change and the legislator will change with the times.

When you look at candidates, the name of the party is not as important as the candidate's agenda. If the course you believe in is to be followed, vote for it.

## You.

It still all comes down to you. As you look around and see what can change and how you can strengthen and legitimize your voice, you will clarify the issues that concern you. Soon you will be able to cut through the innuendo and gloss and see who can best represent you. Your choices may be different from those you originally made.

The more you analyze, the more you can make intelligent, knowing decisions and take the right action for you. You have the tools. Ask the questions and weigh the information before you decide.

*Americans like to talk about (or be told about) Democracy but, when put to the test, usually find it to be an inconvenience. We have opted instead for an authoritarian system disguised as a Democracy. We pay through the nose for an enormous joke-of-a-government, let it push us around, and then wonder how all those a---s got in there.*

**Frank Zappa (1940–1993)**
AMERICAN MUSICIAN, SINGER, AND SONGWRITER

*I know of no safe depository of the ultimate powers of the society but the people themselves; and if we think them not enlightened enough to exercise their control with a wholesome discretion, the remedy is not to take it from them, but to inform their discretion by education.*

**Thomas Jefferson**
(1745–1826)
PRESIDENT OF THE UNITED STATES, 1801–1809

*I find the great thing in this world is not so much where we stand as in what direction we are moving.*

**Oliver Wendell Holmes (1809–1894)**
AMERICAN POET, NOVELIST, ESSAYIST, AND PHYSICIAN.
THE AUTOCRAT OF THE BREAKFAST-TABLE (1858)

# Using Your Voice: Political and Community Activism and Service

## Chapter Seven

# Giving others their voice, *Mesa, Arizona*[1]

"Homeless." "Working Poor." Who are they? **Celeste Lopez** of Mesa, Arizona, knows exactly who they are. Just people—ambitious, talented, imperfect—without the breaks we've had. She's changing that.

To help the living conditions of the migrant worker population, many Mesa families cooked home meals and took them to the orange groves to feed the worker families. Celeste shared this tradition of service with her parents by bringing food to the groves and later, serving meals in soup kitchens and finding living quarters, health care, and opportunity for the working poor and urban homeless of the greater Phoenix area. The dignity of the people she aided made a lasting impression.

Opportunity, she realized, was what most people desired, whether to better themselves financially or to express their needs. Searching within herself to determine how best she could be effective and realizing she could use her high school paper journalism skills, Celeste helped found a community newspaper written and sold primarily by the homeless and working poor within her community.

To start, Celeste researched funding, creating, and printing the newspaper. She had experience writing, but her school publications were already established and funded. Now she was going it alone. She discovered Real Change in Seattle, Washington, a paper with a similar mission. Real Change's founder helped Celeste structure the paper.

Using lawyers and community advisors to ensure that the paper be non-profit and professional, Celeste and several companions got funding and created True Liberty. The paper, first published on July 4, 1997, is a 16-page black-and-white quarterly marketed to the general Phoenix area. In True Liberty the actual voice of the street is being heard, giving contributors the satisfaction of their published expression.

The paper is successful on many levels, influencing civic and societal policies concerning Phoenix's homeless and working poor. Many of Arizona's homeless are now being perceived as gifted writers, artists, and reporters, changing assumptions of what it means to be without a job, residence, or food. The artists and poets of True Liberty are finding confidence and pride in their own innate creative gift. Street vendors are partially supporting themselves with the portion of magazine sales they retain. Others are earning income by serving advertising and business functions for the publication.

*True Liberty* has given rise to opportunities for expression for Celeste and her friends who have realized how opening the door for the unheard supports their own sound. By their efforts, another hurdle standing in the way of regaining and going forward with productive lives is being cleared. Celeste has gone on to college, but the paper she founded remains. She'll vote as soon as she is able, ensuring with that vote that local issues, the ones with which she's been so concerned throughout her life, continue to be effectively and strongly influenced by those who see opportunity in everyone.

*We have too many high-sounding words, and too few actions that correspond with them.*

**Abigail Adams (1744-1818)**
U.S. FEMINIST AND PATRIOT. WIFE OF PRESIDENT JOHN ADAMS AND MOTHER OF PRESIDENT JOHN QUINCY ADAMS.

The bottom line: If you want to make a change for yourself and those you care about, or if you want to preserve what's now that you like, then you must do something.

Voting gives you that most important hold over elected officials and government. But government can't or won't solve all the problems. Some, although significant to us, are too small for government to deal with. Voting, community service, and activism are intensely interrelated, and each can have a direct effect on the other. For example, legislative policy can add or deny support to a social program. Community and social work can carry out the goals of major legislation.

Democracy is participatory. If you want it to work for you, you need to work for it. You can be as conservative, liberal, creative, or weird as you want in figuring out how to get things done. One thing you've plenty of: opinions and energy. If something doesn't look right to you, take an active stand. Find workable solutions or pathways to the solution. To criticize and not act makes you part of the problem.

**Here are some ideas:**

Work alone or with your friends, family, teachers, and others in your community, school, neighborhood, and house of worship. Start to see things through that affect you all. Participate in political campaigns. Work with social action groups. Petition and work for new laws. Push reporters to address problems concerning you directly.

When you find that those in government are waffling on issues important to you, make them face up to their responsibilities. Write to them. Join with others to confront them and make your concerns known. Find interested public officials and let them know that they have your support. Remind them that in a few years you may determine their future directly by your vote.

*I want to have as many opportunities as possible to meet with young people and receive their input on the proposals currently under consideration. The only way we will draft effective legislation is by talking with the kids it will impact.*

**Dan A. Gwadosky**
SECRETARY OF STATE, MAINE, ON TASK FORCE PROPOSALS TO MEET WITH HIGH SCHOOL STUDENTS CONCERNING THE STATE OF MAINE TASK FORCE ON YOUNG DRIVERS (OCTOBER 1997)[2]

Make change by thinking about what you'd like to do and how you might get it done. Remember it doesn't have to be the way anyone else suggests. As you define your issues, apply the questions you ask of others:

★ What is the issue?
★ How does it affect me and those I care about?
★ Can I cut through my bias and that of others to work toward solutions?
★ Do I have enough information?
★ Can I resolve the problem or do I know the road toward a reasonable solution?
★ Will that solution serve us not only now, but in the future?

The most important contribution you can make is to keep your mind open and face what is out there. Always remember your goal.

## Political Campaigns and Government Concerns

If you want to let people know where you and your friends stand and if you want to influence current voters, then formal politics may be the way to go. You can work with politically active individuals and groups. You'll pick up experience in the process that only adds to the resources at your disposal.

Lots of stuff moves slowly and you may be curbing your impatience, counting your yawns and trying not to quit as you find yourself too often in front of the copying machine or getting someone's lunch. Some of the people you work with may be difficult. However, as the campaign or project progresses, you'll find yourself more and more involved in the excitement of it. You're doing this for lots of reasons, including getting a chance to say what you feel and getting involved with policy. And it's exhilarating when something you've worked on starts to suddenly gather momentum and starts making a difference. Go for it!

During an election year, volunteers are at a premium and anything you can offer is gratefully accepted, especially during the summer before major elections when adults still have to work and you may have more free time. Election offices are set up to promote a candidate or an issue. City or county election boards might love to use you for tasks such as distributing registration and voting information to your community or canvassing the neighborhood to get out the vote ("precinct work"). Remember, these may seem unimportant and not terribly scintillating, but they could affect what your parents earn, the quality of your education, or whether your streets get cleaned.

**Helping with Registration and Voting.** This is one way to get as many people as possible out to vote. Whether or not your candidate wins, you have helped with the democratic process—and there is always another election. Here are some ways to participate:

- ★ Distribute registration information and help citizens fill out the forms (check to ensure your state rules permit you to do this).
- ★ See if anyone needs absentee ballots or absentee information.
- ★ Baby-sit for those who need to register and on election day for voters who need to get to the polls.
- ★ If you are bilingual, provide translation services to others in your family or community who have difficulty with English.
- ★ Organize a party or event to highlight voter registration or voting. But be careful. Although you may have heard that others have organized a contest or party that awards prizes or admission to those who bring in registration slips indicating new voter registration or voting poll receipts, federal law broadly construes this as "vote buying"![3]
- ★ Create posters, videos, songs, cartoons, and audio spots to promote registration and voting. Get your work hung at local stores and offices, published in the paper, and aired on local TV and radio. Create a poster contest in your school, your club, or your neighborhood. See if a local business will sponsor it.
- ★ Work with your schools, houses of worship, unions, playgrounds, factories, neighborhood organizations, and local politicians to distribute flyers and general campaign information.
- ★ Make phone or house calls to get voters to the polls and see if you or your parents can drive or accompany those who cannot easily get out to vote.

If aspects of the process seem complicated to you, make suggestions to election boards or officials as to how these procedures can change—not everything is set in stone.

# Garbage Dump Politics
## A TALE OF 7TH GRADE DETERMINATION[4]

It's June of 1998 and the twelfth grade class of Thayer Junior/Senior High School in Winchester, New Hampshire, is graduating. In many of their speeches and senior memories: tales of their seventh grade school year—1992, a presidential election year—when they dramatically changed voter registration statistics in their small town.

In early fall, their teacher read the seventh grade class a Junior Scholastic Magazine article about the low percentage of the "voting age population (VAP)" who actually register and vote. The kids asked, "How many are registered in our town?" They called the town hall. In a town of approximately 5,000 VAP, the numbers were dismal and the big election was looming!

The students had been using **The Giraffe Project curriculum**, a program inspiring kids to "stick their neck out". Adapting the lessons to real work and with great initiative, they planned a voter registration rally to be held on two Saturdays at the four locations where they knew people would show up: the Town Hall, the market, the weekend flea market, and the garbage dump. Kids signed up for a site, asked parents to supervise, created voter information packets and banners, and conducted in-class role-playing scenarios so that they could comfortably answer questions concerning registration. They convinced the home economics teacher to help them make an Uncle Sam costume, which they insisted that their principal wear at the rally points.

Excitement spread through the school and community. Other seventh grade academic teachers suspended their usual lessons to give the students time to get ready. The local radio station announced the drive and the local TV station sent reporters to cover it. The registrar at the Town Hall was called to work with the project.

Then, a snag. There were only three registrars in town and procedural reasons—it hadn't been advertised long enough, there were too many sites and not enough registrars (two had to be present at all times for registration)—were stopping the momentum. Luckily the registrars, seeing what was going on and what it could mean for voting, agreed to hold the registration on the two Saturdays, but only at the Town Hall. Adaptable as always, the class decided to be present at the other three sites to hand out pamphlets and encourage prospective voters to go to the Town Hall.

Registration on the two Saturdays set a town record, including 100 percent registration of the parents of seventh graders. How were they to be graded for the quarter, asked the teacher of the principal? "Any way you want," he said. "A's" for this great lesson in civic participation for the seventh grade, a successful lesson for all involved.

**Working in the campaign:** If there is a candidate or issue you feel strongly about, you may want to work directly.

★Staff campaign headquarters: answer phones, clip newspaper reports on the candidate or issue, type letters and file information, arrange precinct information, help coordinate material distribution and volunteers.

★Form a teen panel/focus group to influence party strategy.

★Distribute campaign literature where you think it would be effective.

★Help decorate the campaign offices, and cars and floats for parades.

★Hand out campaign literature at family and community events.

★Be an usher or a greeter at political events.

★Volunteer as a runner and poll watcher on election day to help determine who is actually voting.

★Create special fund-raising activities to inspire family and friends to support the candidate. You're not as bound to traditional ways as adults, and you may come up with something never before tried!

**Advising others about election issues.** No matter how much homework or chores you have, you still have time to find out what the candidates and propositions really mean. Voting without information can be almost as harmful as not voting at all.

★Take on a project and research it. Then inform voters close to you of the real issues—you may sway their vote.

★Join the youth groups of the DNC and the RNC (Young Democrats, College Democrats, Teen Age Republicans) to learn about the issues and the way a major political party handles them.

★Search out organizations conducting debates of major election issues and/or running mock elections for pre-voters such as the National Parent/Student Mock Election and KidsVoting U.S.A, listed here in the Appendices.

★By yourself or with the help of teachers or your local library, write to government offices and other organizations for data on candidates and issues.

★Pressure civic groups to hold nonpartisan meetings on important issues and use posters, teen pressure, and calm demonstrations to get voters to attend.

**Making laws.** If government isn't taking care of something, it may be that a new law is needed. Work with your community to decide if a new law and its enforcement can best solve the problem.

Contact public officials and make them aware of the issue. Define the issue narrowly and be prepared with facts and arguments supporting the proposal.

Check on the requirements for petitions and then start a valid one among those who will be affected by the change. If you collect sufficient signatures, you may be able to put the proposition on the ballot yourself.

Create fund-raising activities to fund the campaign to pass the law. Use the activities and media to generate financial and public support for the measure.

**After the election.** Just because the excitement is over, our voices needn't be silenced until the next contest. The election is only the beginning. We've encouraged our friends and family to support certain candidates because we were told that these candidates would respond to our needs. It's up to us to follow up.

★ Check with the media about how the politician is handling issues of concern.
★ Check the elected official's local office for the voting record on your concerns.
★ If things aren't going the way you want, start letter-writing and other campaigns to get the official back on track. Sic the media on it by calling the political desk at your local newspaper or TV station.

**Election Reform.** There are ideas flying which could alter our historic political systems while still preserving our democracy. You might want to learn about and get involved with a reform group with exciting new political concepts. Several follow. You can look others up in libraries and on the Internet under "voting reform" or "electoral reform".

> *The short memory of American voters is what keeps politicians in office.*
>
> **Will Rogers (1879–1935)**
> AMERICAN HUMORIST

# Would you work for 16 cents per hour for 12-hour shifts?[5]

Kids in other countries do—to make you the sneakers, clothing, and sports equipment you use everyday.

"Young people need to make our voices heard because we are the number one consumers of products made by children."
**Abby Krasner**, sixteen, of Westminster West, Vermont, is passionately interested in child labor conditions overseas. Realizing that businesses in the United States using overseas labor have been fueling this economy and that issue also concerns U.S. jobs, Abby and the "Progressive Coalition," a club formed at her high school, have carried this concern all the way to the United States Congress. The coalition wrote letter after letter to legislators and to the companies whose products are made with bonded labor

overseas. They started to boycott the products of the U.S. companies who use such labor. With a national student activism alliance, she has collected over 1 million signatures on a petition against sweatshop labor.

Abby has always worked in politics, often volunteering at offices of her U.S. Representative, Bernie Sanders (I, Vermont), when her parents could not. She brought the issue to his office. With the sponsorship of the Congressman, a new law, the first to ban the importation into the United States of products made with bonded child labor, passed in both the House and the Senate.

Unable to avoid the finality of the legislation, and the overwhelming reality of a gigabyte petition, one of the largest

sportswear companies has already announced significant changes in its negotiations with foreign manufacturers, setting a higher minimum age for workers as one of its requirements.

Abby hasn't stopped her activities, though. Child labor still exists and additional legislation and enforcement are needed. Going through the legislative process has given Abby incentive to work on other issues. She is writing a bill to require that the Vermont State Board of Education have at least one high school student member. It already has the support of many members of the legislature as well as the superintendent of the board.

★**Voting Age Reform.** You're 16. You're paying taxes. You're polled by legislators. Your rights are subject to change. How about gaining the right to vote? Several organizations are investigating this issue right now. You might want to check out their reasoning.[6]

★**Campaign Finance Reform.** As long as elections have been held there have been efforts to counteract the influence of money on politics.[7]

★**Multiparty systems** to break up the two-party influence of the Democratic and Republican parties and give powerful and effective power to additional and stable political parties with comprehensive platforms.

★**Proportional Representation** (often allied with multiparty systems) serves to eliminate our "winner-take-all" system.[8] Rather than single seat districts, a district could have several representatives, elected in accordance with the proportion of votes accorded each candidate. Proponents claim it allows for fairer representation of a diverse citizenry, elections run more on issues and less campaign money. It is used by many democracies throughout the world as well as by several local cities and counties in the United States.[9]

★**Instant Runoff Voting (IRV):** In a winner-take-all race, elections will require that the winning candidate win the majority (over 50%) of the vote, however voters will vote for the entire list of candidates, ranking their first, second, and third, etc. candidate choices in order of preference. If the front-runner does not receive a majority, the last place candidate is eliminated and all that candidate's votes move to the voter's next choice. This continues until one candidate wins with a majority of votes, negating the need for expensive run-off elections.[10] It is an election of compromise, much closer to the definition of a purer democratic system.

★**Redistricting:** Where you are located often determines your choice of candidates. Electoral districts are reevaluated and recarved every ten years based upon census, polling, and other statistical information. Redistricting decisions can be political and districts manipulated to influence the outcome of elections. You may want to become involved in the next redistricting efforts to ensure that your vote counts where it is needed.[11]

## Community/World Service

The more we work with others, the more we learn about their needs and the more we refine our own. Two weeks at a Head Start center gives us a better view of the importance of early education than all the reading around. One day helping senior

# Find a Need and Fill it [12]

### SPOKANE, WASHINGTON

Two eleven-year-old sixth graders, **Arielle Ring** and **Valorie Darling**, are making beeswax candles for holiday presents. Both discover that they had cried over a Spokesman-Review pullout section featuring a Romanian trip taken by a local group, accompanied by photos of the horrendous living conditions of orphans there.

At the store on an errand, Arielle and Valorie see candles, beautifully wrapped and very expensive, but no more beautiful than their own. Thus, the creation of Helping Hearts Company. Formed by Arielle and Valorie with several other sixth graders, **Sara Richardson**, **Sara DeCristoforo**, and **Sarah Brogden-Thome,** the girls turned their hobby into a professional nonprofit business, the income to be donated to charities.

Their first step: investigate the charity and the need. They met with the reporter who wrote the Romania article and spoke with the organization sponsoring the trip. Next they pooled their baby-sitting earnings and loans from their parents to purchase wax and packaging.

By letter explaining their business and objective, they canvassed local shops soliciting Christmas orders. Their motto: "It is better to light a candle than to curse the darkness," an old Chinese proverb making reference to the *Spokesman-Review* article's title, "Into the Heart of Darkness." Their professionalism and the quality of their product impressed retailers such as Spokane's best-known restaurant and best department store and orders started flying in. With other friends they worked at least two hours a day packaging two candles with raffia ties and a tag describing Helping Hearts and its intended beneficiary. The girls often personally sold the candles as retailers found them to be their own greatest sales force.

First year sales from Christmas, Valentines Day, and Easter grossed over $10,000 which, after deduction of expenses (including payback of the parent loans) and working capital (this IS a business after all), netted over $7,000 for Romanian orphanages.

The girls look objectively at their enterprise. They research and donate to a different cause each year. Last year it was suicide prevention. Next: possibly hurricane relief abroad, disadvantaged children, or troubled teens. Now thirteen years old, they realize their format will change with time. Among their goals is following their money to where it's been donated, see change, and work further to ensure that it continues to occur. Will they vote? Says Arielle, "[I'll vote] to show I'm responsible, because I care about what's going on, that it works and I know I can make a difference."

citizens at a rest home will open our eyes to the issues of the elderly. Just working positively on a project with buddies will prove the merits of teamwork.

We are a part of the community in which we live. So are others. Just as we don't want them to ignore our voice, we must listen to theirs. Community service provides us the opportunity to work together. In turn, we broaden our outlook. As we start to think seriously about strengthening our voice, community service can give us a base for action. Volunteer for a cause in which you believe. And just because a large organization hasn't gotten behind it doesn't mean it can't be done.

And don't exclude cultural projects. Yes we've been talking "serious" subjects such as education, food, and jobs. But the power to create a visual, literary, dramatic, or musical statement has it's own powerful voice and we want to support institutions and individuals that encourage societal contributions here as well. Check your local guide to what's going on. Take a kid younger than you to a museum or a play.

## Environmental causes:

★Organize your friends, class, or neighborhood to adopt a neighborhood street, park, or stream and be responsible for its cleanup and preservation.
★Point out local pollution problems to the companies responsible as well as to politicians and community agencies.
★Organize carpools for school to reduce fuel needs, exhaust emissions, and traffic congestion.
★Contact local government and corporations to encourage recycling programs.
★Collect recyclable trash from offices and schools and deposit in recycling bins.
★Choose an ecological group that looks good to you. See if you can get your local schools, businesses, or clubs to support it. Offer to create ad material, help in the office, or organize fund-raisers and raffles, even if only among your friends. $5 to $10 adds to all the other $5s and $10s raised.

## Community and human causes:

★Create clothing, book, toy, and food drives for the needy and take the items collected to local shelters. Have a garage sale and give the money to an agency providing food, shelter, clothing, and counseling.
★Volunteer at homeless, abused women, and children's shelters or at hospitals.
★Volunteer to serve food and deliver meals to the homebound.

# Giving Back in **South Central**, Los Angeles, California[13]

Mention South Central and the word "tennis" does not automatically pop into one's head. An expensive, often socially elite game, people of color are not well represented for there are no great clubs, tournament sites, pros, or even enough tennis courts in the area to encourage kids to play. But there have been stellar examples of minority tennis players, and **Katrina Nimmers** of South Central is one of them.

Coached by her tournament tennis-playing father since the age of five, eighteen-year-old Katrina is someone we should watch as she becomes a powerful force in professional tennis. But Katrina's story is not only about tennis, but also about making a change in her community.

South Central has been known for its violence, riots, and other characterizations that do not fit all of the residents, but which hang over all of their heads. Training in tennis requires everyday practice but in South Central, courts are few. To get in the hours, a court was often improvised in a driveway, a backyard, or inside a large building. Even with these difficulties, Katrina wondered why others couldn't also have this opportunity. So, in 1991, at age eleven, Katrina started Tennis on Wheels, a program to provide for others in her neighborhood what she already had: a chance to find a career, learn about oneself, and an alternative to the violence, drugs, and illiteracy faced these days, not only in South Central Los Angeles.

Tennis on Wheels takes its training program everywhere— from the neighborhood public park, to the middle of an asphalt boulevard, to a grassy back road in South Carolina— providing professional tennis instruction to underprivileged youth from two to eighteen for $1 a lesson. It conducts clinics, educational activities, and tournaments involving its participants in the inner cities, providing families there the opportunity to see their children participate and view professional and new players compete. Training and job opportunities are available for teens and adults to coach other kids.

Awakened by Katrina to the possibility of opening new markets in the inner cities, athletic clothing and equipment sponsors are providing racquets, balls, tennis shirts and other items often hard for inner-city families to afford.

Kids are spending time training for a sport that requires focus and determination. Several well-qualified participants, promoted by Katrina and her father to the athletic scouts and sponsors, are now looking at professional tennis opportunities. Others are showing increased interest in their education as a direct result of Tennis on Wheel's requirements of attention to school work as a basis for goals. They are off the streets, and not slouched in front of TV. They are active and resolute. They are all learning how to make changes, within themselves and without.

You get results when you don't give up. Katrina didn't and she's learned how to use her fast-growing celebrity to ensure that others also have a chance.

★Raise money for charities by soliciting pledges for competing in local marathons, bike races, and walk-a-thons.

★Use your friends, teachers, classmates, and family as resources for financial, advisory, and service-oriented contributions.

★Read to children. Read to the elderly.

★Act as counselor, tutor, or mentor for younger children in community, church, or school athletic and other programs.

★Work to provide technology access for your community. Get businesses to donate dollars and computer equipment to schools, libraries, and community centers. See if a local BBS (on-line bulletin board system) can provide access to kids. Teach others (kids and adults, especially retirees) to use the Internet.

★If you must earn money and have no time to volunteer, check out jobs in a community center. Although not well paying, clerking in a neighborhood store may not pay any more and you'll gain knowledge and experience at the center.

★Listen to what you find when you work with social agencies. If things are being messed up, speak up. See if you can create an atmosphere for change. Be prepared not to be listened to because you're young. But know that if you're persistent, have your facts, and show a bit of patience, you will be heard.

## Closest to You—Getting Things Done on Your Block and in Your Neighborhood:

★Join or create neighborhood cleanup and improvement projects.

★Check out what the younger kids in the neighborhood are doing, especially during the hot summer, and see if you and your friends can organize activities, even if only supervising when they rollerblade or bike around the block.

★Help out and check in on older neigbors.

★If there is tension in the neighborhood, get other kids to play and talk together. What you work out can carry back to your parents.

★If there are safety and other concerns, see if you can be a part of organizing the community to find solutions.

★Publish a newsletter on community issues and political concerns. Ask local businesses for free or reduced printing.

★Create a survey of your community on what concerns it. Send results to the residents and businesses, possibly media, and your political representatives.

## Work with your peers and classmates:

★Organize your friends on issues of personal concern to them.
★Connect to youth groups around the country. Many have already learned how to solve problems that affect them.
★Help out at peer support hotlines (or set one up) to help friends and other teens with problems, such as drugs, violence, control of your body, or personal matters that might be easier to discuss with someone your age.
★Create book or T-shirt projects to earn money or create publicity for a cause. Use the resources around you—schools, business, local artists—or find agencies to help you. There are book publishers and foundations, with support money and grants, set up to work with youth ideas.
★See if you can organize a class project around an issue. How far you can carry it in the school and beyond?

# TeenPower a+ Work[14]

It's understandable that, after several fights and one gun incident, the Asheville Mall in Asheville, North Carolina, wanted to protect its customers. But to a group of Erwin High School students the rules imposed by the mall were over the line: No bandannas? No more than four kids could hang together at one time? You had to be with your mom or dad after 6 p.m. on Saturdays if you were under sixteen? Come on. So they took the issue back to the mall.

The mall had made its rules after meeting with "members of the community," but omitted talking to those most affected, some of its most valuable customers. Teens formed an action group and canvassed their fellow students about what seemed to be a better stance, created flyers, and then, with the strength of numbers and purchasing power behind them, set up a series of meetings with the mall.

The mall listened, to not only these voices but to the public outcry the teens engendered when they brought the issue to the general public. While not changing their principal positions (the Saturday evening curfew remained), at least they eased off: deleting the bandanna/clothing restriction and softening congregation restrictions to a rule that a group of kids could not block common areas.

The Asheville teens didn't get everything, but they gained more than they realized: a valid victory for themselves as they expressed their points of view, entered into discussion, and came away with a change.

**James Ale**, age nine, took on the city government of Davie, Florida, seeking a safe, neighborhood park for himself and his friends after he watched a car hit a playmate while playing in the streets, the only open space then available. With petitions, a business card, and a plan, he succeeded in cutting through the bureaucratic red tape (time, size of area and budget, financial allocations) and getting a small pocket park in his neighborhood.[15]

Now in his twenties, James is looking at political office himself.

## Using the Media

You have seen how the media might mislead us if you don't ask enough questions. Yet they are the way in which information gets shared in this country. You can bring them news to publicize things you want done. There is power in truth.

★Take to the media a survey or story about something that concerns you. Be prepared to discuss your concerns. They may be more interested because the information is youth-driven.

★If something can be resolved if more people know about it, call the editorial department of your local newspaper and try to interest a reporter in the story.

*Campaign packaging created during the 1996 presidential campaign by Dreyer's Grand Ice Cream for the western states,* **"Clinton & Cream"** *("smooth but chunky"),* **Cookie Dole** *("the conservative choice with the decidedly unconservative taste"),* **Nutty for Neither** *("Having a hard time deciding. Don't abstain!")*

Articles often bring problem resolution such as citizen funding of a children's baseball league in an inner-city area where the money wasn't there before.

★Write letters to radio and TV programs, and commercial sponsors. Call talk shows. Tell them your age. It helps their demographic statistics and your chances of being heard. Propose a program idea to the producer of local news.

★In your local community, create and distribute booklets about local concerns.

★Many companies create special advertising connecting their products to elections. Contact a company and see how its product can be used for your local campaign. Companies may sponsor events or donate products free or at a discounted rate.

★Use your resources. If you know of family or adult friends with expertise or clout in something that concerns you, get them to participate. With their permission, use their names and reputations to back up your arguments and add weight to your goals. Get them to speak to media on your behalf.

★With your friends and a video camera create a PSA (public-service announcement) and try to get it run on a local radio or TV station.

★Propose a program for the local public-access channel on your cable service.

★Propose a political column to cover kids' concerns in the school or local newspaper. Join or form your own regional teen newspaper or magazine. Several teen-written publications are listed in the Appendix.

★Use the Internet and the various online services to create a web site to put together larger community support and check out others' views. There are many sites already established, including those in the Resource Appendix.

## Educate, Organize, And Protest

Educate and activate those around you. Make them aware that what goes on outside your family and your group of friends isn't just "out there." You are all affected by events taking place in your community, city, or state whether or not you are directly involved. Get them to see.

Bring a group together as a tool for education, public recognition, and publicity. It is difficult to avoid an issue when faced with a large band of calm but concerned citizens who have joined together for what they believe. But know that if the protest gets out of hand, you've messed up.

## Using Your Own Talents

We all have unique talents and our teen years are a significant time to discover the voices we possess. Some of us are natural leaders: captains of football teams, class presidents, head cheerleaders, first in honors classes, teacher/student liaisons. Some are outspoken: debaters, questioners, and prodders of the system. Others are the artists: driving parents loco with amplified guitars, paints strewn in the den, computer graphic skills, cameras, and poetry. Some are quiet, shy. But we all have thoughts and opinions.

The bottom line: Look into yourself and find what it is you can do. Perhaps knowing that you can help make a difference will provide the impetus for the talent you have and its expression will be heard. In gatherings. In one photograph that eloquently tells a story more than words. In a large poster depicting a countdown to registration. In a well-written letter to an editor. In a quiet visit between high-school student and an elementary-school child. Where you make an impression, your voice is heard. It becomes one of change.

Few will have the greatness to bend history itself;
but each of us can work to change a small portion of
events, and in the total of all those acts will be
written the history of this generation.

**Senator Robert F. Kennedy (1925–1968)**
"DAY OF AFFIRMATION" ADDRESS,
UNIVERSITY OF CAPETOWN, SOUTH AFRICA, JUNE 6, 1966

# A Fable for Living in Los Angeles, California[16]

Los Angeles is known for its palm trees silhouetted against blue sky. It is also known for its smog. During summer, it makes the sky gray and your eyes and lungs hurt. Smog can hurt more than that as well.

Over twenty-five years ago, **Andy Lipkis** escaped L.A. to a camp in the nearby San Bernardino mountains. But L.A. was closing in. The trees there were dying due to pollution. Government wasn't planning on replanting and the forest was going to be gone by 2000. But Andy had heard that there were smog-resistant trees. "Why can't we plant these trees to replace the dying

ones?" he asked his camp counselor who answered, "You can't replant a whole forest."

But Andy Lipkis thought he could. From the age of twelve, Andy worked on political campaigns, doing the things that young kids do: car washing among them. He learned how to get things done. Now fifteen, he knew he could save his forests.

Starting with that first camp, Andy and two dozen campers selected a deforested parkland acre that had been polluted with oil and destroyed by smog and other pollutants over the years. They removed the layers of soil, let it breathe and started their first planting. Within three weeks, the area was again alive.

Over the next three years, not without frustration and failures, Andy enlisted twenty camps in his tree project. He heard that the State of California was selling 20,000 surplus smog-resistant baby trees for $600, an amount few kids have. The state refused to donate them, even though they were scheduled to be destroyed. Andy employed his favorite motto, "Failure isn't failure. It's compost for success," and moved into high gear.

Using his young political experience, Andy called two lawmakers and the *Los Angeles Times* and told them of the hundreds of camp kids ready to help the environment. The lawmakers investigated. The *L.A. Times* published an article suggesting that kids donate at least fifty cents each toward the program.

Within a day after the article's publication,

Andy's mailbox was overflowing with letters containing donations, most of them in the fifty cents range. Within three weeks, he had collected $10,000. Although the state had plowed under 12,000 of the trees by the time the *L.A. Times* article ran, significant interest in the issue woke politicians up to the large constituency Andy had unearthed and the state was stopped from destroying the remaining trees and they were donated to Andy's cause. Andy still needed to get the trees to the hillsides. Kids and companies donated empty milk cartons to hold each small sapling, people power to pack them in the cartons, refrigerated space to keep them cool (some in an ice cream store and Andy's college dorm cafeteria), and transportation to get them to the hills.

In the meantime camp kids, already involved and ready to fight for what they believed in, wrote letter upon letter to the governor of California, saying essentially, "The forest is dying. What are you going to do about it?" As a result, the legislature allocated financial support for reforestation programs all over the state. The Department of Forestry was ordered to give away any future surplus trees to nonprofit groups rather than destroy them.

Using the donations, Andy and his supporters started "The Tree People," named after what people called them. First focusing on reforestation and preservation, Andy enlisted campers and other kids to plant the trees and created environmental education programs to teach kids why a forest dies and how to save it. Within the next twenty years, Tree People became the nation's largest environmental education program, working with middle and high school students and over 100,000 elementary school kids.

Under Andy's continuing leadership, Tree People has been significantly involved in creating citywide recycling programs for Los Angeles by teaching kids (who in turn educate their parents) about saving the earth. He is now working on changing this highly developed city into an urban forested watershed ecosystem, providing better oxygen and simple poetic relief from the urban density.

A major city is undergoing dramatic environmental change for the better. By joining with other environmental/tree groups throughout the world and creating the Citizen's Forestry Movement, the concerns of just one teen have developed over the years into a strong and forceful movement to take back our earth.

Does Andy vote? "I have always voted, and don't believe I've ever missed an election since I turned eighteen. . . . [it] is critical. We . . . teach kids all about the fact that even if they can't vote they can still communicate with the people who are their legislators. [It's] one of the key ways to make things happen."

*We need to respect our differences and hear them, but it means instead of having shrill voices of discord, we need a chorus of harmony. In a chorus of harmony you know there are lots of differences, but you can hear all the voices.*

**William Jefferson Clinton (1946– )**
**PRESIDENT OF THE UNITED STATES (1993–2001)**

# Coda

To encourage others to hear you, you have to know the right words. Give them meaning. Choose them properly. String them together with passion and understanding and you create a powerful voice for yourself. In chorus with others, you can reshape our world.

"And when I reach voting age?" In a changing, growing democracy many issues will arise that will concern us all. Everything you've done for yourself, your family, your friends, and community is only a part of the picture. With enabling legislation and the right representatives, you can make truly significant change. Remember you are responsible for those in office. You can support or critique them. You can even be one of them.

Using all the power you now have plus that last and potent power of the vote, your voice will resound in the concert stadiums of public life. Register. Inform. Vote. It's your stage. It's your world. There is no longer any excuse not to be in it.

# Resource Appendices

There are zillions of ways to find information about political and social issues, and to get involved. Explore the activism resources to find political information and better known national advocacy organizations, many with chapters in your area. Some magazine and award competitions may inspire you. Information sites can educate you and help you educate your community of friends, parents, and teachers. Look also at the sources in the Bibliography, especially books like *The Kids Guide to Social Action* and *Generation React: Activism for Beginners*.

Think of key words that can give your research direction, including "voting," "political action," "teen involvement," "community activism," "voting rights," "human rights," "civil rights," "environment." You'll think of a lot more. Use your media literacy tools as you research anything—some of the site descriptions are their own.

# Source Notes

**Preface**

1. U.S. Census Bureau, "Resident Population Estimates of the United States by Age and Sex: April 1, 1999 through August 1, 1999".
   http://www.census.gov/population/estimates/nation/intfile2-1.txt

**Chapter 1**

1. Robin Benedick, staff writer, "Teen Curfews: Help or Hindrance?," *Sun Sentinel*, South Florida, 1998.
2. "ACLU Brings First Federal Challenge to Drug Testing of Students in Academic Courses," ACLU press release, Wednesday, August 18, 1999
   http://www.aclu.org/news/1999/n081899a.html.
3. Interview with Andy Lipkis, Summer 1998.
4. Interview with Sarah Swagart, July 1998, "Giraffe Profiles," The Giraffe Project. http://www.giraffe.ord/swagart.htm.

**Chapter 2**

1. Information adapted from "Integrated Instruction: Making the Connections," Kathleen R. Nelesen, M.Ed., Planning Interdisciplinary Activities, Urban Middle School, Sheboygan, Wisconsin ©1998 Kathleen R. Nelesen.

**Chapter 3**

1. We the People: The Citizen and the Constitution (1995), Center for Civic Education, Calabasas, CA (a joint project of the Center for Civic Education, funded by the United States Department of Education by act of Congress).
2. Burke Davis, *Black American Heroes of the American Revolution*, New York, Harcourt Brace Jovanovich, 1976.
3. Carole Lynn Corbin, *The Right to Vote* (Issues in American History), New York, Franklin Watts, 1985.
4. "Fellner and Mauer, Human Rights Watch, "Losing the Vote: The Impact of Felony Disenfranchisement Laws in the United States" (1998). http://www.hrw.org/reports98/vote.
5. There are steps which can be taken to regain the vote, however most ex-felons are not informed of the availability of this process, nor do they have the political nor financial resources to seek it. Ibid.
6. Joe Loya, "A Man with No Vote" San Jose Mercury News, Sunday May 31, 1998
7. Justice Policy Institute and The Children and Family Justice Center (Northwestern University), Second Chances http://www.cjcj.org/centennial
8. "Voting Rights Act," "The American Presidency," Grolier Online, http://gi.grolier.com/presidents/aae/side/voterite.html.
9. Corbin, Carole Lynn, *The Right to Vote* [Issues In American History], Franklin Watts, New York/London/Toronto/Sydney, 1985
   Lindop, Edmund, *The First Book of Elections,* New York, Franklin Watts, Inc., NY 1968
10. Federal Elections Commission, 1998 http://www.fec.gov/pages/agedemog.htm.
11. As of this printing, tabulation of the percentage of votes in the 1998 Congressional elections has not been completed and the 2000 election not yet held. For a list of the number of total primary & general '98 election votes by state: http://www.fec.gov/pubrec/fe98/pgalchart.htm.
12. Interviews with Laura Beth Moore, Summer 1998
    The 1993 Giraffe Annual, The Giraffe Foundation, Langely, WA

## Chapter 4

1. Interview with David Levitt, Summer 1998, The Giraffe Project, Langely, WA., "The Teen Action Awards," react magazine, a division of Parade, http://www.react.com/activate/take_actions_awards/runners.html. State of Florida House Bill 105/Senate Bill 466, *Seminole Times*, Wednesday, June 24, 1998, an edition of the *St. Petersburg Times*.
2. Courtesy of Doubleday, a Division of Random House, Inc.
3. Based upon League of Women Voter materials, Los Angeles, 1996
4. *San Francisco Chronicle*, April 23, 1998 (Tanya Schevitz); *San Francisco Examiner*, April 21–23, 1998 (Bernice Yeung); www.sfgate.com
5. Conversations with Tom Richey and Teen Age Republicans (1996),Washington, D.C.
6. Conversations with Cecilia-Nan Ding, Summer 1998, Quote from F.A.S.T. press release, Boston, Mass. Information provided by Teen Action Awards, react magazine, a division of Parade, http://www.react.com/activate/take_actions_awards/runners.html#ding; New York, NY
   *The Daily Free Press*, December 11, 1997
   *Time,* December 1997
   *The Boston Phoenix,* August 15, 1997
   TAB, March 10-16, 1998

## Chapter 5

1. *San Gabriel Valley Tribune,* West Covina, CA., August 13, 1997
   *Student Press Law Center Report*, V.XIX, No 1, Winter 1997
   *ACLU News,* June 17, 1997, American Civil Liberties Union.
2. Paul Robeson, "We can't sit out this election," *Freedom* (1952)
3. Conversations with Justin Kopetsky, May 1998
4. Interview with James "Ryan" Mitchell, 1998, "Teen Action Awards" (Ryan was a runner-up), react magazine, a division of Parade, New York, NY. http://www.react.com/activate/take_actions_awards/runners.html#ding,
   "Information Pamphlet" Election Division, Office of the Secretary of State, State of North Dakota.
5. http://www.alp.org.au/herald/jfjuly97.htm.
6. Naomi Bernstein, Director of Communications, New York City Board of Elections, New York, NY. June 1998.
7. Samuels, Cynthia K., *It's a Free Country! A Young Person's Guide to Politics and Elections*, Atheneum, New York (1988).
8. Pitts, David, "Third Parties Score Limited Success in U.S.," Issues of Democracy, USIA Electronic Journals, Vol. 1, No. 13, September 1996, http://usiahq.usis.usemb.se/journals/itdhr/0996/ijde/thirdpe.html
9. Academic American Encyclopedia, "The Whig Party," Grolier Online: The American Presidency, http://gi.grolier.com/presidents/aae/side/whig.html. Academic American Encyclopedia, "The Democratic Party," Grolier Online: The American Presidency, http://gi.grolier.com/presidents/aae/side/dparty.html
10. Information adapted from "U.S. Party Resource Page" Political Science Department, Western Michigan University (January 1997), http://www.wmich.edu/politics/resources/party.html & http://www.wmich.edu/politics/resources/thirdpar.html.
11. Margaret Rosenfield, "Early Voting," National Clearinghouse on Election Administration, Federal Election Commission, Washington, D.C. (April, 1994).
    "Voting Machines: Project V.O.T.E. Curriculum," The Office of the Secretary of State, State of Texas (1995).
    Conversations June 1998 with Joyce L. Wright, Director, Kent County Department of Elections, State of Delaware, Dover, DE. October, 1998 with:
    (1) Karen Koyne, Election Specialist, Office of Election Administration, Federal Election Commission, Washington, D.C.
    (2) Polli Brunelli, Director, Federal Voting Assistance Program, Washington, D.C.
    (3) Kathryn Ferguson, Registrar of Voters, Clark County, Nevada
    (4) Kim Sutton, Director, Project V.O.T.E., Office of the Secretary of State, State of Texas.
    "History of the Voting Machine," Sequoia Pacific Voting Equipment Press Materials (1998), http://www.spve.com/products/history_of_the_voting_machine.html.
    "Why Voting Machines in Lieu of Paper Ballots" (1998), Sequoia Pacific Voting Equipment Press Materials, http://www.spve.com/products/why_voting_machines.html.
12. Conversations October 1998 with Polli Brunelli, Director, Federal Voting Assistance Program, Washington, D.C. David Maidenberg, "Using the Internet in Election Offices," Office of Election Administration, Federal Election Commission, Washington, D.C. (April, 1998).
13. Michelle Koidin, "Mir Astronaut Will Become First American to Vote from Space," Associated Press, October 29, 1997.
14. Jennifer Warren, "Voters Seem to Enjoy Chance to Shop Around," *Los Angeles Times,* June 3, 1998.
15. "Rules of the Republican Party," Adopted 1996 at the Republican National Convention (governing delegate selection for the 2000 Presidential Election).

16. "Call for the 2000 Democratic National Convention," Democratic Party of the United States, (draft September 19, 1998).
   "Delegate Selection Rules for the 2000 Democratic National Convention," Democratic Party of the United States, 9 May 1998.
17. "How to participate in the 1996 Delegate Selection Process," Office of Party Affairs & Delegate Selection.
   Terry Michael, "The Democratic Party's Presidential Nominating Process. 3rd Ed. (1995)," Pamphlet of the DNC written by the Exec. Director, Washington Center for Politics and Journalism & former press Secretary, DNC.
18. "The Electoral College and the National Archives and Records Administration," Federal Register, January 7, 1998, http://www.nara.gov/fedreg/ec-artcl.html.
   "A Procedural Guide to the Electoral College," The Office of the Federal Register, January 12, 1988, http://www.nara.gov/fedreg/proced.html.
   "Presidential Electors," Election Division, Indiana Secretary of State, http://www.state.in.us/iec/html/electors.html.
   Pika et al, The Presidential Contest 4th Ed. (1992).
19. List Of States And Votes National Archives and Records Administration, URL:http://www.nara.gov/fedreg/96ecvote.html.
20. "Electoral College Box Scores," National Archives and Records Administration, Federal Register, http://www.nara.gov/fedreg/ec-boxsc.html.
21. Interview with Molly Madden, Spring 1998. Information provided by react magazine and "Teen Action Awards" (Molly was a '98 winner), http://www.react.com/activate/take_actions_awards/madden.html.

## Chapter 6

1. Paraphrasing from Back to Methuselah ( 1921) by George Bernard Shaw (1856-1950). "You see things; and you say 'Why?' But I dream things that never were; and I say 'Why not?'" Respectfully quoted, ed. Suzy Platt, Barnes & Noble Books, NY (1993) and their source: Public Papers of the Presidents of the United States, John F. Kennedy, 1963 p. 537.
2. Conversation with Lauren Gaffney, June 1998 react magazine, a division of Parade, New York, NY (Lauren was a "Take Action" runner-up 1998) http://www.react.com/activate/take_actions_awards/runners.html#ding Kids CAN, http://www.kids-can.org, the Kids Care AIDS Network web site.
3. Information for this section is based on and adapted from brochures from the Center for Media Literacy, Los Angeles;

"Citizenship in a Media Age (Media Literacy and the Common Good)," 1996 National Media Literacy Conference, Los Angeles October 3–5, 1996); KidsVoting USA; Media Literacy: Resources & Activities, New Mexico Media Literacy Project, New Mexico State Department of Education; Kids & TV: A Parent's Guide to TV Viewing, Cablevision, Charlotte, NC and "Our Kids & Teens Magazines" and Center for Media and Values, Los Angeles.
4. Antonio Gonzalez quoted in The New York Times, "In Los Angeles, Quandary for Hispanic Voters," Seth Mydans, Friday, June 2, 1995.
5. Conversations, February 1998 with Deborah Edwardson, author and journalist, Barrow, Alaska.
6. Excerpt from "A Poet's Advice to Students," copyright © 1955, 1965 by the Trustees for the E. E. Cummings Trust. Copyright © 1958, 1965 by George J. Firmage, from A Miscellany Revised by E. E. Cummings, Edited by George J. Firmage. Reprinted by permission of the Liveright Publishing Corporation.
7. Media materials, Center for Media Literacy, Los Angeles, CA. Project V.O.T.E. Curriculum, Office of the Secretary of State, Texas
   "The Debates: Image vs. Substance," Better Viewing, Continental Cablevision, September/October 1996.

## Chapter 7

1. Interviews with Celeste Lopez & Eva Lopez 1998, "Teen Action Awards" (Celeste was a winner), react magazine, a division of Parade, New York, NY, http://www.react.com/activate/take_actions_awards/lopez.html.
2. 1997 Press Releases from the Maine Department of the Secretary of State: Dan Gwadosky, Secretary of State www.state.me.us/sos/what1997.htm#houiaes.
3. 42 U.S.C. (United Sates Code) 1973 i(e): "This statute applies in all jurisdictions . . . also prohibits 'vote buying' in the broadest terms possible by forbidding any 'payment' or 'offer of payment' that is made to a would-be voter 'for voting' or to induce unregistered individuals to get on the electoral roles. A 'payment' encompasses anything of material value including lottery chances."
4. Interview, June 1999 with Stephanie Brodie, seventh grade teacher, Thayer Junior/Senior High School, Winchester, New Hampshire.
5. Interviews with Abby Krassner, 1998; Interview with Phil Faiermonte, Outreach Programs at the Office of Congressman Bernard Sanders (I, Vermont), June 1998; react magazine, (Nancy Vittorini, June 15 - 21, 1998), New York;

Rutland Herald, Vermont;
Press releases on the "Sanders Amendment to House Treasury Bill," 1997; New York Times; Associated Press.

6. http://www.thehilltimes.ca/hilltimes/youth.html;
http://peterstwp.com/teenboard/messages/35.html;
http://www.studentactivism.org.

7. "According to the Center for Responsive Politics, during the 1996 election cycle, in House races the candidate who raised the most money won 92 percent of the time; in the Senate, 88 percent. Given such a direct correlation between campaign spending and electoral success, it's less than surprising that illegal fundraising scandals have plagued both parties. As a result, a majority of American voters now believe that major changes should be made in the way election campaigns are financed, raising hopes that a new and more promising era of campaign finance reform has arrived." EPN (Electronic Policy Network) Briefing Book, http://epn.org/camfinre.html.

8. "There is a broad range of PR systems. Some are based on voting for political parties; others for candidates. Some allow very small groupings of voters to win seats; others require higher thresholds of support to win representation. All promote more accurate, balanced representation of the spectrum of political opinion in a given electorate."
"What is Proportional Representation?," The Center for Voting and Democracy, http://www.fairvote.org/pr/intro.htm.

9. "What is Proportional Representation?," The Center for Voting and Democracy, http://www.fairvote.org/pr/intro.htm.

10. "Instant Runoff Voting (IRV):A Fairer Way to Conduct Single-Winner Elections." The Center for Voting and Democracy http://www.fairvote.org/irv/a_fairer_way.htm.

11. "Elections and Redistricting" National Conference of State Legislatures,
http://www.ncsl.org/programs/legman/elect/reso11.htm.
"Problems with Political Redistricting" University of Buffalo, http://www.geog.buffalo.edu/ucgis/UTopic_redistrict.html.
"Common Causes issue" Reapportionment and Redistricting:
http://www.ccsi.com/~comcause/position/pp_rr.html.

12. *Spokesman-Review,* Spokane Washington, articles 11/21/96 & March 26, 1997;
The Giraffe Society, Langely, WA.
Interview with Arielle Ring, June 1998.

13. Conversations with Katrina Nimmers and Michael Nimmers June, 1998;
Press release for "Tennis on Wheels," Los Angeles, CA.
*Los Angeles Times,* February 27, 1996.

14. *USA Weekend,* May 2–4 , 1997;
Conversation with Michael Ruby, Director of Security, Asheville Mall, Asheville, North Carolina June 1998;
*Asheville Citizen Times.*

15. Giraffe Society, Langely, Washington;
Hoose, Philip, *It's Our World, Too!,* Little Brown and Company, (1993).

16. Tree People press materials
Conversation with Andy Lipkis, Founder of the Tree People, June 1998

# Resource Sites for Activism, Election and Government Information, and Issues

Almost everyone's jumping on the Internet, but if you wish to speak or write to a real person, there are phone numbers and addresses here too! Note: the "http://" usually doesn't need to be typed into Explorer or Netscape for the World Wide Web to take you to a site, so just the "www" of the URL is here.

**The Book Site:  www.teenpowerpolitics.com**

The web sites are current to the last moment before publication, but may change as web sites often do. Check here for up-to-date issues, resources, and links

## GETTING STARTED
**American Civil Liberties Union (ACLU)**
www.aclu.org/
125 Broad Street, 18th Floor, New York, N.Y. 10004-2400
Information and advocacy on everyone's rights. Check the student's rights section.

**America Online**
For those of you who are subscribers, check out their keywords.

**Amnesty International**
www.amnesty.org/
322 8th Ave, New York, NY 10001
(212) 807-8400
Worldwide campaign to promote human rights.

**Center for Policy Alternatives**
www.cfpa.org
1875 Connecticut Avenue, NW, Suite 710, Washington, D.C. 20009
(202) 387-6030
Community-based solutions. "Youth Voices" is a survey of issues of 18–24 year olds.

**Children's Defense Fund**
www.childrensdefense.org
25 E Street NW, Washington, D.C. 20001
(202) 628-8787
cdfinfo@childrensdefense.org
Education about the needs of children and encourages preventive investment in youth.

**Children's Rights Information Network (CRIN)**
www.crin.org
A global network of organizations sharing information on children's rights.

**The Giraffe Project**
www.giraffe.org/giraffe/
PO Box 759, Langley WA 98260
(360) 221-7989 fax (360) 221-7817
Publicizing and inspiring people who stick their necks out for the common good.

**Joint Center for Political and Economic Studies**
www.jointcenter.org/
1090 Vermont Ave. NW, Suite 1100 Washington, D.C. 20005-4961
(202) 789-3500 fax (202)789-6390
Health facts on African American youth and an African American history checklist

**League of Women Voters of the United States**
www.lwv.org/
1730 M Street, NW Washington, D.C. 20036-4508
(202) 429-1965 fax (202) 429-0854 lwv@lwv.org
Encouraging informed and active citizen participation in government.

**The National Women's History Project**
www.nwhp.org
7738 Bell Road, Windsor, CA 95492
(707) 838-6000 fax (707) 838-0478
Materials to recognize and celebrate women's diverse lives and contributions to society.

**Teen Hoopla (An Internet Guide for Teens)**
http://www.ala.org/teenhoopla/
YALSA, pretty cool teen librarians, packed this site full of great information, reading, and issue forums and links to what you and others feel about what interests you.

**Third Millennium**
http://thirdmil.org/
Focusing on long-term problems with a stated goal "to inspire young adults to action."

**Youth Info**
http://youth.os.dhhs.gov/youthinf.htm
Find out your numbers: male or female, TV habits and other important topics.

**The White House Project**
www.thewhitehouseproject.org
110 Wall St., 2nd Floor New York, NY 10005
admin@thewhitehouseproject.org
Celebrating women's leadership in American politics and mobilizing women to participate in civic life.

**Who Cares**
www.whocares.org
1436 U Street NW, Suite 201 Washington, D.C. 20009
(202) 588-8920 fax (202) 588-8920
A magazine to help people create, grow, and manage organizations for the common good.

GENERAL GOVERNMENT & POLITICAL CONTACTS AND INFORMATION

**CapWeb: the Internet Guide to the US Congress**
www.capweb.net
Congressional and judicial contacts, a newsletter on Capitol Hill happenings and congressmen's political views. Archives some historic presidential debates.

**Constitution of the United States of America**
www.access.gpo.gov/congress/senate/constitution/conart.html (Constitution)
www.access.gpo.gov/congress/senate/constitution/conamt.html (Amendments)
Official text of the Constitution & Amendments. A slow download.

**Documents Center**
(University of Michigan)
http://henry.ugl.lib.umich.edu/libhome/Documents.center/
A central reference point for local, state, federal, or foreign government information.

**E-The People**
www.e-thepeople.com
Send a letter or a petition to over 140,000 federal, state, and local officials.

**The Electronic Activist**
www.berkshire.net/~ifas/activist/index.html
An activism "how to" and e mail directory of Congress, state governments, and media.

**The Jefferson Project**
www.voxpop.org:80/jefferson/
A comprehensive guide to on-line political information.

**Master List of Web Pages for the Members of Congress:**
House of Representatives: www.house.gov
Senate: http://www.senate.gov/contacting/index.cfm
U.S. official government publications: www.access.gpo.gov
Catalogues and indices to official publications of the U.S. government.

**U.S. Government Agencies Info**
www.lib.lsu.edu/gov/fedgov/html

**U.S. Government Documents**
ftp.spies.com
nova.cc.purdue.edu
Famous speeches, inaugural addresses, and laws farther back even than the Constitution!

**Write Your U.S. Representative**
www.house.gov/writerep/
Contact information by the office of each Member of the House of Representatives.

## ELECTION & VOTER INFORMATION

**The Center for Responsive Politics**
www.opensecrets.org
1320 19th Street NW, Suite 620 Washington, D.C. 20036
(202) 857-0044 fax (202) 857-7809 info@crp.org
Tracks and reports on money in politics, and its effect on elections and public policy.

**Center for Voting and Democracy**
www.fairvote.org
6930 Carroll Ave., Suite 901
Takoma Park, MD 20912
(301) 270-4616 fax (301) 270-4133 cvdusa@aol.com
New democratic election systems to encourage increased participation and fairness.

**The Democracy Center**
www.dnet.org/
An opportunity to check and compare positions of candidates and elected officials.

**ElectNet**
www.electnet.org
www.electnet.org/updates.qry
A comprehensive guide to election, current issues, and recent election results.

**Election Map Bank**
www.worldmedia.fr/elections
Info about United States elections.

**Federal Elections Commission**
www.fec.gov
999 E. Street NW Washington, D.C. 20463
(800) 424-9530
The real source: information on campaign finance; elections & voting.

**Federal Voting Assistance Program: State Primaries and Elections Guide**
www.fvap.ncr.gov
FVAP, Department of Defense
1155 Defense Pentagon, Washington, D.C. 20301-1155
(800) 438-8683
For military and civilian members of the armed services. Good info guides for everyone.

**First Vote**
www.closeup.org/frstvote.htm
44 Canal Center Plaza, Alexandria, VA 22314-9836
(888) 256-7387
A high school classroom based program on voter education, registration, and citizenship.

**KidsVoting USA**
www.kidsvotingusa.org/
398 South Mill Avenue, Suite 304, Tempe, Arizona 85281
(602) 921-3727 fax (602) 921-4008
Student members work for voter education among kids. A K-12 classroom curriculum.

**Latino Vote 2000**
http://www.starmedia.com/latinovote2000/
A Spanish-language website for voters.

**National Coalition on Black Voter Participation**
www.bigvote.org
Issues concerning and increasing the rolls of African American voters in the United States.

**National Student/Parent Mock Election**
www.azstarnet.com/~nspme/main.html
225 West Oro Valley, Tucson, AZ 85737
fax (520) 742-3553
Community education and election projects nationwide for kids.

**Politically Black.com**
http://www.politicallyblack.com
A leading website for minority politics with a special section for young voters.

**Power the Vote**
www.lhj-lwv.com/
Good info on candidates.

**Project Vote Smart**
www.vote-smart.org/
One Common Ground, Philipsburg, MT 59858
(888) VOTE SMART
One of the best sites! Incredible resource for candidates, issues, and election information.

**Rock the Vote**
www.rockthevote.org/
10635 Santa Monica Boulevard, Box 22, Los Angeles, CA 90025
(310) 234-0665
Founded by the music industry to bring youth power to the vote. Has online registration.

**Skeleton Closet**
www.realchange.org/
"All the Dirt on All the Candidates — Because character DOES matter." Weird but leading to legitimate questions about all the candidates.

**Southwest Voter Registration Education Project & The William C. Velasquez Institute**
www.wcvi.org/svrep.htm
403 E. Commerce, Suite 220, San Antonio, TX 78205

(800) 404-VOTE fax (210) 222-8474
Educating and promoting the vote in the Latino community.

**Web White & Blue**
www.webwhiteblue.org
Links to some of the best online election directories and voter info sites.

**WhiteHouse 2000**
www.niu.edu/newsplace/whitehouse.html
Links to a wealth of news stories, potential candidates, issue and other information about the presidential campaign for the year 2000.

**Women's Voting Guide**
www.womenvote.org/
Compare your positions with current U.S. senators and representatives and candidates.

P A R T I E S
Several links for major political parties and established or upcoming third parties. Look at sites such as Politics 1 (below) or under "U.S. political parties" for others.

**Democratic National Committee**
www.democrats.org/index.html
430 S. Capitol St. SE, Washington, D.C. 20003
(202) 863-8000
The home page for the Democratic Party.

**Green Party USA**
www.greens.org/gpusa/
PO Box 1134, Lawrence, MA 01842
(978) 682-4353 gpusa@igc.org

**Labor Party**
www.labornet.org/lpa/
PO Box 53177, Washington, D.C. 20009
(202) 234-5190 fax (202) 234-5266

**Libertarian Party USA**
http:www.libertarian.org
2600 Virginia Avenue NW, Suite 100
Washington, D.C. 20037
(202) 333-0008 fax (202) 333-0072

**Politics 1**
www.politics1.com/
450 E. Las Olas Boulevard, Suite 800, Fort Lauderdale, Florida 33301
(954) 768-5368 fax (954) 523-7002
Links and descriptions of most U.S. political parties.

**Reform Party**
www.reformparty.org
P.O. Box 9, Dallas, Texas 75221
Phone (972) 450-8800 fax (972) 450-8821

**Republican National Committee**
www.rnc.org/
310 First Street, SE, Washington, D.C. 20003
(202) 863-8500 fax (202) 863-8820 info@rnc.org
The official site of the Republican Party.

## Media Literacy and the Press

**The Advertising Educational Foundation, Inc.**
www.aded.org/
220 East 42nd Street, Suite 3300, New York, NY 10017-5806
(212) 986-8060
Whether advertising makes people buy things they don't need. An industry funded site.

**Asian American Journalist Association**
www.aaja.org/front.html
1765 Sutter St., Suite 1000, San Francisco, CA 94115
(415) 346-2051.
Promoting accurate news coverage of Asian American issues. Aid to future journalists.

**Center for Media Literacy**
www.medialit.org
4727 Wilshire Blvd., Suite 403, Los Angeles, CA 90010
(323) 931-4177 fax (323) 931-4474
One of the first places to find out what's really going on with messages we're receiving.

**The Freedom Forum & Newseum**
www.freedomforum.org/
The Newseum: 1101 Wilson Blvd, Arlington, VA
(888) NEWSEUM
Satellite gallery: 580 Madison Ave. in New York City
(212) 317-7596
Visit the Newseum, the only interactive museum of news

**Just Think**
www.justthink.org/
Promoting media literacy, critical thinking, and creating one's own messages.

**Unity: Journalists of Color, Inc.**
www.aaja.org/front.html
An alliance of underrepresented minority journalist associations and diverse perspectives.

## General Service & Advocacy

Look first at these national programs but you can also search out state and local groups more directly aligned with your interests. Remember you can also start your own!

**Americorps Project**
www.americorps.org/americorps.html
1100 Vermont Avenue NW, Washington, D.C. 20525
(800) 942-2677
Earn help paying for education in exchange for a year of community service.

**Boy Scouts of America**
www.bsa.scouting.org/
1325 Walnut Hill Land, P.O. Box 152079, Irving, Texas 75015-2079
(214) 580-2000
The Venturing Program matches programs to the interests of young people (14–20).

**Campaign for America's Future**
www.ourfuture.org
1025 Connecticut Avenue NW, Suite 205, Washington, D.C. 20036
(202)955-5665 fax (202) 955-5606 info@ourfuture.org
Progressive change by sparking a robust national debate about America's future.

**Database**
www.react.com/activate/take_actionDB/index.html
Service opportunities keyed to your interests by gender, age, state and other information.

**The Democracy Center**
www.democracyctr.org/
P.O. Box 22157 San Francisco, CA 94122
(415) 564-4767 fax  (978) 383-1269
Advocacy training for global social and economic justice. A good training manual.

**DO Something: Young People Changing the World**
www.dosomething.org/
423 West 55th Street, 8th Floor, New York, NY 10019
(212) 523-1175 fax (212) 582-1307
mail@dosomething.org
AOL Keyword: Do Something
Great site for the tools you want to take action. Check out their opportunities.

**Girl Scouts of America**
www.gsusa.org/
420 Fifth Avenue, New York, NY 10018
(212) 852-8000
Just for Girls has info not only for scouts and connections worldwide to GirlGuides.

**Girls Incorporated**
www.girlsinc.org/
30 East 33rd Street, New York, NY 10016
(212) 689-3700
Teaches girls (6–18) how to advocate for themselves. Annual summer training program.

**International Student Activism Alliance (ISAA)**
www.studentactivism.org/
A student-run organization for high school students tackling teen issues such as early school starting times, curfews, censorship, and student representation.

**National Council of La Raza**
www.nclr.org/
1111 19th NW, Suite 1000, Washington, D.C. 20036
(202) 785-1670
Supporting Hispanic community-based organizations in urban and rural areas.

**National Council of Negro Women, Inc.**
www.ncnw.com
633 Pennsylvania Ave. NW, Washington, D.C 20004
(202) 737-0120 info@ncnw.com.
Uniting African American women, the umbrella for widely diverse organizations.

**National Urban League**
www.nul.org
120 Wall Street, New York, NY 10005
(212) 558-5300
Political and social action, a job bank, and links to other African-American interest sites.

**Nickelodeon's Big Help**
www.nickelodeon.com/
PO Box 2626, New York, NY 10108
Their Big Help campaign gives you a chance to make a difference in your community.

**Points of Light Foundation**
www.pointsoflight.org/
1735 H Street NW, Washington, D.C. 20006
(202) 260-5749
Former President George Bush's project for volunteers in community service.

**ServeNet**
www.SERVEnet.org
The premier website on service. Find volunteer opportunities across America by zip code.

**Student Leadership Network for Children (SLNC)**
www.childrensdefense.org/slnc1.html#what
A national network of servant-leaders, ages 18 to 30, committed to positive social change.

**Youth In Action Network**
www.mightymedia.com/youth/
c/o Mighty Media 400 1st Avenue N., Suite 626 Minneapolis, MN 55401
(800) 644-4898
An interactive online service about positive social action and service projects.

**F.A.S.T. (Friends and Shelter for Teens)**
59 Temple Place, Suite 512, Boston, MA 02111
(617) 542-FAST fax (617) 542-3270
Cecilia Nan-Ding's company to fight and educate youth about domestic and teen dating violence.

**Kids Care AIDS Network**
www.kids-can.org/
Lauren Gaffney's organization to unite young people to fight against HIV/AIDS.

**Tennis On Wheels**
746 E 89th Street, Los Angeles, CA 90002
(213) 750-0514
Contact Katrina Nimmers to see what's going on and where with Tennis on Wheels.

**The Tree People**
12601 Mulholland Drive, Los Angeles, CA 90210
(818) 753-4600 fax  (818) 753-4625 Treepeople@igc.apc.org
Andy Lipkis makes it a personal responsibility to save our community and forests.

**USA Harvest**
(800) 872-4366

**Voices of Struggle**
PO Box 2031
Berkeley, CA  94702
(510) 893-3181 x124 fax  (510) 893-5362
Organizing primarily in California to challenge education cuts and massive prison spending, anti-immigrant backlash and include ethnic studies classes in school.

C I V I C   &   C O M M U N I T Y
**America's Promise: The Alliance for Youth**
www.americaspromise.org
909 North Washington Street, Suite 400, Alexandria, VA 22314-1556
(703) 684-4500 fax  (703) 535-3900
Join with General Colin Powell to help children, youth, and their families nationwide.

**Boys and Girls Clubs of America**
www.bgca.org/
1230 W. Peachtree Street NW, Atlanta, GA 30309
(404) 815-5700 lmclemore@bgca.org
Inspiring kids to realize their full potential as productive, responsible, and caring citizens.

**Camp Fire Boys and Girls**
www.campfire.org/
4601 Madison Ave., Kansas City, MO 64112-1278
(816) 756-1950
Great citizenship and non-partisan political activity programs.

**Center for Civic Education**
www.civiced.org
5146 Douglas Fir Road, Calabasas, California 91302
(818) 591-9321
Civics materials for civic participation, helping kids identify issues and find solutions.

**Food Not Bombs**
www.webcom.com/~peace/PEACTREE/stuff/stuff/HOMEPAGE.html
3145 Geary Blvd. Suite 12, San Francisco, CA 94118 (415) 386-9209
Vegetarian free food action organization for food distribution, education, and advocacy.

**Girl Power**
www.feminist.com/girls
A great list of links for girls, including activism sites and magazines.

**Habitat for Humanity**
www.habitat.org/how
121 Habitat Street, Americus, Georgia 31709
(912) 924-6935 fax  (912) 924-6541
public_info@habitat.org
Former President Jimmy Carter leads the way. Habitat for Humanity is known for enlisting everyone, young and old, to build homes in disadvantaged areas.

**Literacy**
There are community projects everywhere helping adults and children learn to read or reading for the blind and elderly. Call any public library and volunteer.

**Reading is Fundamental, Inc.**
www.rif.org/
Toll Free: (877) RIF-READ
Children's and family literacy programs that help prepare young children for reading and motivate school-age children to read.

## HUMAN RIGHTS, CIVIL RIGHTS

**Americans for a Society Free from Age Restrictions**
www.asfar.org/
Youth's civil rights: the voting age, curfew, & other laws limiting their freedom.

**Anti-Defamation League/A World of Difference Peer Training Program**
www.adl.org
823 United Nations Plaza, New York, NY 10017 (212) 885-7700
Advocating an environment for different voices and fighting against racism, prejudice, stereotypes, homophobia, anti-Semitism, and discrimination.

**The American-Arab Anti-Discrimination Committee (ADC)**
www.adc.org/mission.html
4201 Connecticut Ave N.W, Suite 300, Washington, D.C. 20008 USA
(202) 244-2990 fax (202) 244-3196
ADC@adc.org
Defending the rights of people of Arab descent and promoting their rich cultural heritage.

**The Center for Juvenile and Criminal Justice**
http:www//cjcj.org
2208 Martin Luther King Jr. Ave SE, Washington, D.C. 20020
(202) 678-9282 fax (202) 678-9321
Working for a more reasoned system of justice, including juvenile justice.

**Gay, Lesbian Straight Education Network (GLSEN)**
www.glsen.org/
(212) 727-0135 fax (212) 727-0254
A leading voice for equality, safety, value, and respect for all in the educational system.

**Human Rights Watch**
www.hrw.org/
350 Fifth Avenue, 34th Floor New York, NY 10118-3299
(212) 290-4700 fax (212) 736-1300
hrwnyc@hrw.org
Protecting human rights around the world and bringing offenders to justice.

**Indian People's Action,**
A chapter of Montana People's Action
http://mtpaction.org
208 East Main Street, Missoula, MT 59802
(406) 728-5297
Bringing youth and the many Native American tribes together to combat discrimination in schools, jobs and opportunities

**Equity in Sports**
www.arcade.uiowa.edu/proj/ge/
Investigating gender equity in interscholastic or intercollegiate sport.

**National Association for the Advancement of Colored People (NAACP)**
http://www.naacp.org/
(410) 521-4939 (Information Hotline)
Our oldest, largest and strongest civil rights organization. Non-violent advocacy for political, educational, social and economic rights of minorities.

**National Conference for Community and Justice (NCCJ)**
www.nccj.org/
71 Fifth Avenue, 11th Floor, New York, NY 10003
(212) 545-1300 fax  (212) 545-8053
Ongoing community awareness aimed at eradicating bias, bigotry, and racism.

**National Organization for Women**
www.now.org/
733 15th St NW, 2nd floor, Washington, D.C. 20005
(202) 628-8NOW
Bringing women into full participation in the mainstream of American society.

**National Youth Advocacy Coalition**

www.nyacyouth.org/

1638 R St. NW, Suite 300, Washington, D.C. 20009

(202) 319-7596 fax (202) 319-7365

Advocating for and with young gay, lesbian, or transgender people to end discrimination.

**Southern Christian Leadership Conference (SCLC),**

334 Auburn Ave NE, Atlanta, GA 30312

(404) 522-1420  fax (404) 659-7390

Non-profit, non-sectarian, inter-faith advocacy for social, economic, and political justice.  Organized following the 1957 Montgomery bus boycott by the Reverends Martin Luther King, Jr., and Ralph Abernathy, among others.

**Southern Poverty Law Center**

www.splcenter.org

400 Washington Avenue, Montgomery, Alabama 36104

Legal advocate against white supremacist and hate groups. School materials.

C H I L D R E N

**The Black Community Crusade for Children**

www.childrensdefense.org

25 E Street NW, Washington, D.C. 20001

(202) 662-3797 fax (202) 662-3580

Freedom Schools concerns school meals, after-school activities, mentors, and role models.

**Children Now**

www.childrennow.org

1212 Broadway, 5th Floor, Oakland, CA 94612

(510) 763-2444      fax  (510) 763-1974

children@childrennow.org

Great on-line center for child activists.

**Coalition for America's Children**

www.usakids.org/

A huge coalition of organizations and individuals working for America's kids.

**National Child Rights Alliance**

http://home.att.net/~alexist/ncra/frames.htm

Directed entirely by youth and adult survivors of abuse and neglect.

**Stand for Children**

www.stand.org/

1834 Connecticut Avenue NW Washington, D.C. 20009

(800) 663-4032 fax (202) 234-0217

Identifies, trains, and connects local children's activists.

**UNICEF**

www.unicef.org

UNICEF House, 3 United Nations Plaza, New York, N.Y. 10017

(212) 686 5522  fax  (212) 867 5991

One of the great children's rights and health status worldwide organizations.

E N V I R O N M E N T   &   A N I M A L S

**Alliance for Community Trees**

www.treelink.org/connect/orgs/act/about.htm

201 Lathrop Way, Suite F, Sacramento, CA 95815

(800) ACT-8886 fax (916)924-3803

The national network for grassroots groups dedicated to tree planting and conservation.

**American Oceans Campaign**

http://americanoceans.org/ca/net/

725 Arizona Avenue, Suite 102, Santa Monica, CA 90401

(310) 576-6162 fax  (310) 576-6170

Educating public and legislators on marine policy and the value of our unpolluted oceans.

**Center for Environmental Citizenship**

www.envirocitizen.org.

611Connecticut Ave. NW, #3-B, Washington, D.C. 20009

(202) 234-5990  fax (202)234-5997

Programs: Campus Green Vote, National Environmental Wire for Students, EarthNet, Blueprint for a Green Campus, Summer Training Academy, Internship Program.

**Humane Society of the United States**

www.hsus.org

2100 L St. NW, Washington, D.C. 20037

(202) 452-1100

Campaigns against pet overpopulation, unnecessary animal testing, and animal protection.

**The Nature Conservancy**
www.tnc.org/
4245 North Fairfax Drive, Suite 100, Arlington VA 22203-1606
(703) 841-5300
"Nature's real estate agent." Preserving habitats and species by buying, protecting, and managing lands and waters they need to survive using a business real property model.

**Rainforest Action Network**
www.ran.org
221 Pine Street, Suite 500, San Francisco, CA 94104
(415) 398-4404 fax (415) 398-2732 rainforest@ran.org
Activism and education for Earth's rain forests and the rights of their inhabitants.

**Sierra Student Coalition**
http://ssc.org/
P.O. Box 2402, Providence, RI 02906
(401) 861-6012  or (888) JOIN-SSC
The student-run grassroots network within the Sierra Club moving the student agenda.

**US Environmental Protection Agency/EPA Student Center**
www.epa.gov/students/
401 M Street SW, Washington, D.C. 20460
(202) 208-5634
Education materials on pollution and other issues affecting our environment

**World Wildlife Fund**
www.wwf.org
1250 24th Street, NW, Washington, D.C. 20037
(202) 293-4800
Protects wildlife, wetlands, and rain forests in Latin America, Asia, and Africa.

P O L I T I C A L
**The Association for Children's Suffrage (ACS)**
www.brown.edu/Students/Association_for_Childrens_Suffrage/
College and high school students challenging the voting age.

**Black Youth Vote**
www.bigvote.org
Increasing voter participation and politically empowering African American youth.

**College Democrats Home Page**
www.democrats.org/college_democrats/
430 S. Capitol Street SE, Washington, D.C. 20003
(202) 863-8000
Yes it's college, but they welcome younger members.

**Young and College Republicans**
www.crnc.org/
600 Pennsylvania Ave. SE, Suite 302, Washingon, D.C.  20003
(202) 608-1417
The Republican Party's youth affiliates on campus and elsewhere.

**Common Cause**
www.commoncause.org/
1250 Connecticut Avenue NW, Washington, D.C. 20036
(202) 853-1200
Seeking a unified voice against corruption in government and money special interests.

**National Teenage Republican Headquarters (TARS)**
www.teenagerepublicans.org
PO Box 1896, Manassas, Virginia 22110
(703) 368-4214     fax (703)368-0830
The teen organization for the  Republican National Committee.

**Youth Speak**
www.oblivion.net/youthspeak/
A grass-roots, youth run, youth led, youth empowerment organization.

**Young Democrats of America**
www.democrats.org/yda/
430 S. Capitol Street SE, Washington, D.C. 20003
(202) 863-8000
The official youth arm of the Democratic Party.

**Youth In Government Program (YMCA)**
www.ymca.net
101 N. Wacker Drive, Chicago, Illinois 60606
(800) USA-YMCA
A huge hands-on mock legislative program. An annual youth conference in Washington, D.C.

## H E A L T H   &   S A F E T Y
**Advocates for Youth**
www.advocatesforyouth.org
Information for responsible decisions about their sexual and reproductive health.

**Crisis Hotlines:**
For use and for helping others by volunteering.
Use keywords: "teen crisis hotline" "teen hotline" "youth hotline" "youth crisis."

**The American Red Cross HIV/AIDS Teen Hotline**
www.redcross.org
(800) 440-8336
A peer-to-peer HIV/AIDS education program and crisis referral plus volunteer program.

**Anti-tobacco education and activism**
www.tobaccofreekids.org
www.kickbutt.org
www.no-smoke.org

**Elizabeth Glaser Pediatric Aids Organization**
www.pedaids.org/
2950 31st Street, #125, Santa Monica, CA 90405
(310) 314-1459 fax  (310) 314-1469
The leading U.S. national non-profit organization concerning pediatric HIV/AIDS.

**FDA (Federal Drug Administration) Kids Home Page**
www.fda.gov/oc/opacom/kids
Teens and preteens can learn about FDA-related subjects.

**Join Together**
www.jointogether.org/
Grassroots efforts to end gun violence and substance abuse in America.

## E D U C A T I O N
One of the best ways to help others and make change: help yourself!

**American College Entrance Directory**
www.aaced.com
Info, links, virtual walking tours of thousands of colleges, scholarships, etc.

**Embark.com**
www.embark.com/ugrad.asp
Info on 6,000 two and four-year institutions; careers and majors; and financial aid.

**Occupational Outlook Handbook**
www.stats.bls.gov/ocohome.html
Job descriptions, salaries, education or certification requirements.

**PowerStudents.com**
www.powerstudents.com/
Check out both their "High School" and "College" sections for pragamatic and real info.

**SAT Program**
www.collegebaord.org/sat/html/students/indx001.htlm
School codes, application deadlines, practice questions, college essay advice.

## Leadership Training

**American Legion: Americanism and Children & Youth Programs**

www.legion.org

P.O. Box 1055, Indianapolis, IN 46206

(317)630-1200  fax (317) 630-1223

Girls State/Girls Nation, Boys State/Boys Nation, Americanism and Children and Youth.

**ASPIRA Association, Inc.**

(202) 835-3600

Leadership development and education for Puerto Rican and other Latino youth.

**Close Up Foundation**

www.closeup.org/home.htm

44 Canal Center Plaza, Alexandria, VA 22314-1592

(800)  256-7387

Giving students and adults a "close up" look at government, including Capitol tours.

**Co-ette Club**

2020 West Chicago Blvd., Detroit, Michigan 48206

(313) 867-0880

Community involvement and leadership skills for African-American high school girls.

**4-H Youth Development**

www.4-h.org

At first just for kids who lived on farms, but now expanded to include so much more.

**Mountain States Network Against Bigotry**

(303) 839-5953

The summer American Youth Leadership Institute, trains youth to make informed decisions against bias and other hate issues. Molly Madden trained here.

## Teen Journalism & Debate Opportunities

Search under **"teen magazines," "school newspapers"** to find the most up-to-date listings of magazines. Be careful, however, since the search engines are not that discriminating.

**Cultural Horizons**

www.odata.se/hotel/friab/dream.htm

An international student magazine written by and for youth worldwide.

**First Cut Magazine**

www.firstcut.com/

An award-winning weekly teen magazine show with stories by teen field correspondents.

**In the Mix**

www.pbs.org/wnet/mix/

Speaking out about the unique experiences of teens worldwide with youth reporters.

**JINN/Pacific News Serivce**

www.igc.org/pacificnews/jinn/toc/4.22.html

"A biweekly online magazine with "the chicken's eye view" because we look at the world from two feet off the ground—through the lens of culture rather than politics."

**Libertarian Rock**

www.libertarianrock.com/

459 Columbus Avenue, Suite #258, New York, NY, 10024

Provides news coverage and commentary about libertarian teens.

**National Student Press Association/Student Media Sourcebook**

http://studentpress.journ.umn.edu/sourcebook.html

Organizations and resources that help student journalists and journalism teachers.

**NewsWeb**

www.nvnet.k12.nj.us/newsweb/

Information sources for student journalists, listings by state of online school newspapers.

**Student Press Law Center**

www.splc.org

1101 Wilson Blvd., Suite 1910, Arlington, VA 22209

(803) 807-1904

The only legal aid agency devoted exclusively to educating and litigating for high school and college journalists about the First Amendment rights and responsibilities.

**TechnoTeen**

www.TechnoTeen.com/teen/index.html

**Teen Issues Message Board**

www.injersey.com/msgboard/Issues/Social/Teen/0002.html

An email posting process to post or get response to issues that concern you.

**Yahoo's list of online school (K-12) and street newspapers**

(with teen contributions)

www.yahoo.com/News_and_Media/Newspapers/K_12/

www.yahoo.com/Society_and_Culture/Issues_and_Causes/Poverty/Homelessnesss/Street_Newspapers/

OTHER NEWS, POLITICAL & TEEN RELATED MEDIA SITES

**Atlantic Unbound/Politics**

www.theatlantic.com/atlantic/election/connection/

The Atlantic Monthly's online magazine with lots of in-depth and current political news.

**CNN: All Politics**

http://cnn.com/ALLPOLITICS/

CNN's political pages online. Election news and related stories, including Time articles.

**Democracy Now**

www. igc.org

A positive place for dialogue, questioning, informational exchange, and activism.

**The Doonesbury Electronic Town Hall**

www.doonesbury.com/

The freshest, hand-sorted political news and analysis with a twist and chat halls.

**horizon Magazine**

www.horizonmag.

**Junior Scholastic Interactive**

www.scholastic.com/jsi/index.htm

For grades 6–8 covering latest news, with an archive of stories from the magazine.

**Kids' Wall Street News**

www.kwsnews.com

National news and financial publication for kids.

**NewspaperLinks.com**

www.newspaperlinks.com/

The "ultimate newspaper portal," for U.S. daily and weekly newspapers on the Web.

**Politics Now**

www.PoliticsNow.com/

Election news from ABC, National Journal, Washington Post, LA Times, & Newsweek. The Weekly Reader-election coverage for kids.

**Radio Free Europe**

www.rferl.org/

The classic source for global radio programming concerning human rights and liberty.

**react**

www.react.com

Pretty cool teen news site plus the Take Action Database with great activism links.

**Teen People Online**

www.pathfinder.com/teenpeople

Teen People's blend of issues and trends, real teens, and celebrities.

**USA Today**

www.usatoday and www.USAweekend.com/

Check out their election site and compare what each candidate says to other candidates. An annual survey for students in grades 6 through 12 on a topic of importance.

**The New York Times UPFRONT**
www.nytimes.com/upfront
The first news magazine designed specifically for teenagers.

**The Wall Street Journal Classroom Edition: Student Center**
http://info.wsj.com/classroom/Student/Student.html
Good links to economics, politics, consumer, child labor, and student issues and newspapers, including The CIA World Factbook.

## A W A R D S
It's great when your work is rewarded and can draw funding and publicity to your cause!

**Do Something BRICK Award for Community Leadership**
www.dosomething.org
or at America Online, Keyword: Do Something
423 West 55th Street, 8th Floor, New York, NY 10019
Annually honors ten outstanding leaders (under 30) who strengthen their communities.

**Do Something Grants**
www.dosomething.org
423 West 55th Street, 8th Floor, New York, NY 10019
or at America Online, Keyword: Do Something
Provides funding up to $500 for people (under 30) who want to build their community.

**Children's Summit Competition/Disney Adventures**
www.disney.com/ChildrensSummit
P.O. Box 6127, Burbank, CA 91510-6127
(800) 728-0430
For kids from 7–14 who design a volunteer project to help their communities "grow up"

**The Giraffe Project**
PO Box 759, Langley, WA 98260
(360) 221-7939
Individuals can nominate someone who "sticks their neck out" to get something done.

**NewsCurrents Student Editorial Cartoon Contest**
PO Box 52, Madison, WI 53071
Original cartoons (K-12th grades) on subjects of national or international interest.

**Skipping Stones**
PO Box 3939, Eugene, OR 97403
(541) 342-4956
International ompetition for creative writing and artwork promoting multicultural awareness, peace and nonviolence.

**react Take Action Awards**
www.react.com
Honoring kids between 12 and 18 years old who have not yet entered college and who have made outstanding contributions to their communities, the nation, and/or the world.

## R E F E R E N C E   S I T E S
**Biographical Dictionary**
www.s9.com/biography/

**Black History Month**
Spotlight Feature blackhistory.eb.com

**Encyclopedia Britannica Online**
www.eb.com/

**Global Vision Human Rights Map Browser**
www.igc.apc.org/globalvision/docs/hr-map/map-frame.html

**Grolier's on-line site: The American Presidency**
www.grolier.com/presidents/preshome.html

**The National Women's History Project**
www.nwhp.org/

**Stately Knowledge**
www.ipl.org/youth/stateknow/skhome.html

**The Virtual Reference Desk**
www.virtualref.com/

**Vote Smart Web Yellow Pages**
www.vote-smart.org/about/services/publications/vswyp97/

KINDA FUNNY/INTERESTING SITES

If you have nothing else to do, you might glean some information along the way!

**The Fig Bar Man Presidential Campaign**
www.epix.net/~wayne26/mrfigb/figbar.html
"Some may laugh. Some may scoff. But Fig Bar Man vows to be your next President!"

**Comedy Central**
www.comcentral.com
Political news with a sense of humor.

**Chupacabra/Alf Campaign**
http://chupa.addiction.com/
Includes a theme song and write-in information.

**Phoebe for President**
www.cbsnews.com/camp96/Phoebe/phoebe_home.htm
The presidential campaign of a fictional teenage girl.

**Who for President????**
www.globaldialog.com/~larryt/preswho.htm
Slork, the alien, promises not to eat you and to vaporize the deficit if elected.

**World's Smallest Political Quiz**
www.self-gov.org/quiz.html

# Bibliography

Angelou, Maya. *On The Pulse of Morning*. New York: Random House, 1993.

Augarde, Tony, ed. *The Oxford Dictionary of Modern Quotations*. New York/London: Oxford University Press, 1991.

Baker-Fletcher, Karen. *A Singing Something: Womanist Reflections on Anna Julia Cooper*. New York: Crossroad, 1994.

Barone, Grant Ujifusa & Michael. *The Almanac of American Politics* (published biannually). New York: Random House, 1996.

Bennett, William J. *The De-valuing of America*. New York: A Touchstone Book, 1992.

Bernards, Neal. *Population: Detecting Bias*. Greenhaven Press, Inc., CA. 1992.

Carrel, Annette. *It's the Law: A Young Person's Guide to Our Legal System*. Volcano, CA: Volcano Press, 1994.

Center for Civic Education. *We The People Series*. CA: Center for Civic Education, 1995.

City Kids. *City Kids Speak on Prejudice*. New York: Random House, 1994.

Cloward, Frances Fox Piven and Richard A. *Why Americans Don't Vote*. New York: Pantheon Books, 1988.

Corbin, Carole Lynn. *The Right to Vote* [Issues in American History]. New York: Franklin Watts, 1985.

Davis, Burke. *Black Heroes of the American Revolution*. New York/London: Harcourt Brace Jovanovich, 1976.

de Toqueville, Alexis. *Democracy in America* New York: New American Library, 1991.

Donaldo, Smith and Davison Mesner, ed. *The NY Public Library Book of 20th Century American Quotations*. New York: Warner Books, 1992.

Elections Division, Texas: Office of the Secy. of State. *Project V.O.T.E. Texas Curriculum*. Texas: Office of Secy. of State, Texas, 1998.

Elshtain, Jean Bethke. *Democracy On Trial*. New York: BasicBooks (HarperCollins) 1995.

Erickson, Ph.D., Judith B. *1998–1999 Directory of American Youth Organizations* (updated). MN: Free Spirit Publishing, 1998.

Fradin, Dennis B. *Voting and Elections*. Chicago: Children's Press, 1985

Fritz, Jean. *Shh! We're Writing the Constitution*. New York: G.P. Putnam's Sons, 1987.

Fritz, Jean.. *You Want Women to Vote, Lizzie Stanton?* New York: Putnam, 1995.

Giovanni, Nikki. *Racism 101*. New York: William Morrow & Company, 1994.

Greenberg, Ellen. *The People's Guide to Congress*. Dobbs Ferry, NY: The Streamside Company, 1996.

Goodman, Alan (Nickelodeon). *The Big Help Book*. New York/London/Sydney/Toronto/Singapore: Pocket Books, 1994.

Hakim, Joy. *War, Peace, and All That Jazz*. New York: Oxford University Press, 1995.

Hakim, Joy. *The New Nation*. New York: Oxford University Press, 1993.

Hewett, Joan & Richard. *Getting Elected: The Diary of a Campaign*. New York: Lodestar Books/E.P.Dutton, 1989.

Hirsch, Jr., E.D & F. Kett, James Trefil. *The Dictionary of Cultural Literacy*. Boston: HoughtonMifflin, 1993.

Hollender, Jeffrey. *How To Make the World a Better Place*. New York: Quill/William Morrow, 1990.

Hoose, Phillip. *It's Our World, Too!* Boston/Toronto/London: Little, Brown and Company, 1993.

Jackman, Michael. *Crown's Book of Political Quotations*. New York: CrownPress, 1988.

Katz, Mark. *I Am Not A Corpse*. New York: Dell Publishing, 1996.

Lappé, Francis Moore & Paul Martin DuBois. *The Quickening of America*. SF: Jossey-Bass, Inc. Publishers, 1994.

Lewis, Barbara A. *The Kid's Guide to Social Action*. MN: Free Spirit Publishing, 1991.

Lindop, Edmund. *By A Single Vote!* PA: Stackpole Books, 1987.

Lindop, Edmund. *The First Book of Elections*. New York: Franklin Watts, 1968.

Loeb, Jr., Robert H. *Your Guide to Voting*. New York/London: Franklin Watts, 1977.

Maisal, Sandy, ed. *Political Parties and Elections in the United States*. New York: Garland Publishing, 1992.

Paine, Albert Bigelow. *Thomas Nast, His Period and His Pictures*. Princeton, NJ: The Pyne Press, 1904.

Panzer, Ed, and the National Museum of American Art. *Celebrate America: in Poetry and Art*. New York: Hyperion Books for Children, 1994.

Partnow, Elaine. *The New Quotable Woman*. New York: Facts On File, 1992.

Peavey, Linda S. & U. Smith. *Women Who Changed Things*. New York: Scribner, 1983.

Phillips, Louis. *Ask Me Anything about the Presidents*. New York: AvonCamelot, 1992.

Pika, Zelma Mosley, Richard A. Watson, Joseph A. *The Presidential Contest*, 4th ed. Washington, D.C.: CQ Press, 1992.

Platted, Suzy. *Respectfully Quoted*. New York: Barnes & Noble Books, 1993.

Provensen, Alice. *The Buck Stops Here: The Presidents of the US*. New York: HarperTrophy, 1990.

Ravitch, Abigail and Diane Thernstrom. *The Democracy Reader*. New York: HarperCollins, 1992.

Riley, Dorothy Winbush, ed. *My Soul Looks Back, Less I Forget*. New York: HarperCollins, 1993.

Ruben, Nancy. *Ask Me If I Care: Voices From An American High School*. Berkeley: Ten Speed Press, Berkeley, 1994.

St. Hill, *Thomas Nast*. New York: Dover Publications, Inc., 1974.

Samuels, Cynthia K. *It's A Free Country! A Young Person's Guide to Politics & Election*. New York: Athenuem, 1988.

Scholastic Magazine Teacher's Ed. *Election '94 Guide to Candidates & Issues*. Scholastic Magazine, 10/7/94.

Schwartz, Alvin. *The People's Choice*. New York: E.P. Dutton & Co, Inc., 1968.

Seuling, Barbara. *The Last Cow on the White House Lawn & Other Little Known Facts About the Presidency*. New York: Doubleday & Co, Inc., 1978.

Severn, Bill. *The Right to Vote*. New York: Ives Washburn, Inc., 1972.

Terry, Michael. "The Democratic Party's Presidential Nominating Process." Washington, D.C.: Wash. Ctr. for Politics & Journalism, 1996.

Thomsett, Michael C. Thomsett & Jean Freestone. *Political Quotations: A Worldwide Dictionary*. NC: McFarland, Jefferson, 1994.

Thoreau, Henry David. *Walden, Civil Disobedience & Other Essays* (1946). New York: Dover Thrift Editions, 1992.

Zimmerman, Richard. *What Can I Do to Make a Difference*. New York: Plume/Penguin Group, 1992.

"Call for the 2000 Democratic National Convention." Washington, D.C.: Democratic Party of the United States, 1998.

"Delegate Selection Rules for the 2000 Democratic National Convention." Washington, D.C.: Democratic Party of the United States, 1998.

*Early Voting: Innovations in Election Administration*. Washington, D.C.: National Clearinghouse on Election Administration, 1994.

"The Electronic Transmission of Election Materials: Innovations in Election Administration." Washington, D.C.: National Clearinghouse on Election Administration, 1994.

*Editorial Cartoons by Kids*. WI: Zino Press, WI (Published annually 1989–Present)

*"Losing the Vote: The Impact of Felony Disenfranchisement Laws in the United States"* (1998) Jamie Fellner, Human Rights Watch & Marc Mauer, The Sentencing Project www.hrw.org/reports98/vote/.

"National Standards for Civics and Government" (Pamphlet). CA: Center for Civic Education, 1994.

"Reinventing Citizenship?" Kettering Foundation, Winter 1994 Review (513)434-7300.

"Rules of The Republican Party (Delegate Selection for 2000)." Washington, D.C.: Republican National Committee, 1996.

National Clearinghouse on Election Administration D.C. 1995.

"Using the Internet in Election Offices: Innovations in Election Administration." Washington, D.C.: Office of Election Administration, Federal Election Commission, 1998.

Vote Smart Web *Yellow Pages*. Project Vote Smart, Or.

## Further Reading
### CIVICS & COMMUNITY INFO AND ACTIVITIES

Carter, Jimmy. *Talking Peace: A Vision for the Next Generation*. New York: Dutton Books, 1993.

The Earth Works Group. *50 Simple Things You Can Do To Save The Earth*. Berkeley, CA.: Earthworks Press, 1989.

Javna, John & The Earthworks Group. *50 Simple Things Kids Can Do to Save the Earth*. Andrews & McNeel, 1990.

Kalergis, Mary Motley. *Seen & Heard: Teenagers Talk About Their Lives*. New York: Stewart, Tabori & Chang, 1998.

Katella-Cofrancesco, Kathy. *Children's Causes; Celebrity Causes*. Brookfield, CT: Twenty-First Century Books, 1998.

King, Jr. Martin Luther. *"I Have A Dream", The quotations of Martin Luther King, Jr.* (ed. Lotte Hoskins). New York: Grosset & Dunlop, 1968.

Langston, Thomas S. *With Reverence and Contempt: How Americans Think About Their President*. Johns Hopkins University Press, 1995.

Lewis, Barbara A. *Kids with Courage: True Stories About Young People Making A Difference*. MN: Free Spirit Publishing, 1992.

———. *The Kids' Guide to Service Projects*. MN: Free Spirit Publishing, 1998.

Lincoln, Abraham. *(A House Divided 1858) Speeches & Writings 1832–1858 & 1858–1865* (2 vols.). The Library of America, 1989.

McVey, Vicki. *Planet Care & Repair*. San Francisco: Sierra Club Books for Children, 1993.

Maestro, Betsy & Giulio. *The Voice of the People: American Democracy in Action*. New York: Lothrop, Lee & Shepard Bks., 1996.

Miles, Betty. *Save The Earth: An Action Handbook For Kids*. New York: Alfred A Knopf, 1991.

Mitchell, Michelle. *A New Kind of Party Animal: How the Young Are Redefining Politics As Usual*. New York: Touchstone/Simon & Schuster, 1998.

Pedersen, Anne. *The Kid's Environment Book; What's Awry and Why*. John Muir Bk., Santa Fe, NM/Norton Books: 1991.

Schwartz, Linda. *How Can You Help? Creative volunteer projects for Kids Who Care*. Santa Barbara, CA: The Learning Works, Inc., 1994.

Seo, Danny. *Generation React: Activism for Beginners*. New York: Ballentine Books, 1997.

Sheer, Jurate Kazickas & Lynn. *Susan B. Anthony Slept Here: A Guide to American Women's Landmarks*.

Walker, Samuel. *Hate Speech: The History of an American Controversy*. Lincoln NE: University of Nebraska Press, 1994.

Zeinert, Karen. *Free Speech: From Newspapers to Music Lyrics*. NJ: Enslow Publishers, 1995.

———. *250 Ways to Make America Better*. George Magazine, Villard Books, NY 1999.

———. *Artistic Freedom Under Attack*. Washington, D.C.: Periodic Reports People For The American Way, 19xx.

———. *Directory of American Youth Organizations: Guide to over 400 clubs, Groups, etc*. MN: Free Spirit Publishing, 1998 (updated).

### ELECTIONS & POLITICS

Cunningham, Liz. *Talking Politics: Choosing the President in the Television Age*. Praeger/Greenwood Pub. Group, 1995.

Dunnahoo, Terry. *How To Win A School Election*. New York: Franklin Watts, 1989.

Hess, Stephen. *The Little Book of Campaign Etiquette*. Washington, D.C.: Brookings Institution Press, 1998.

Lewis, Michael. *Trail Fever*. New York: Alfred A. Knopf: 1997.

McCully, Emily Arnold. *The Ballot Box Battle*. New York: Alfred A. Knopf, 1996.

Smith, Betsy Covington. *Women Win the Vote*. NJ: Silver Burdett Press, Inc., 1989.

Vidal, Gore. *The American Presidency*. Odonian Press, 1996–1998.

## FILMS

Most films are studio. Check your library and online for those harder to find.

*A Perfect Candidate*, documentary, 1995.

*Advise and Consent*, 1962.

*All the President's Men*, 1976.

*Being There*, 1979.

*Bob Roberts*, 1992.

*Boys N the Hood*, 1991.

*Broadcast News*, 1987.

*Bulworth*, 1998.

*Canadian Bacon*, 1994.

*Citizen Kane*, 1941.

*Countdown to Freedom*, documentary, 1994.

*Cry Freedom*, 1987.

*Dave*, 1993.

*Dr. Strangelove*, 1964.

*Election*, 1999.

*First Monday in October*, 1980.

*Get on the Bus*, 1996.

*Ghosts of Mississippi*, 1996.

*Malcolm X*, 1992.

*Medium Cool*, 1969.

*Mississippi Burning*, 1988.

*Mr. Smith Goes To Washington*, 1939.

*My Fellow Americans*, 1996.

*Nixon*, 1995.

*Norma Rae*, 1979.

*Pack of Lies: The Advertising of Tobacco*, documentary, 1998.

*Primary Colors*, 1998.

*Roger & Me*, documentary, 1989.

*Separate but Equal*, 1990.

*Seven Days in May*, 1964.

*State of the Union*, 1948.

*Tennessee Johnson*, (bio of Andrew Johnson, 17th President), 1942.

*The American President*, 1995.

*The Best Man*, 1964.

*The Burning Season: The Chico Mendez Story*, 1994.

*The Candidate*, 1972.

*The Imagemaker*, 1984.

*The Man*, 1972.

*The People vs. Larry Flynt*, 1996.

*The President's Analyst*, 1967.

*The Road Warrior*, 1981.

*The War Room*, documentary, 1993.

*Tito and Me*, 1992.

*True Colors*, 1990.

*Wag the Dog*, 1997.

*Wild in the Streets*, (What if the voting age were lowered to 14?), 1968 .

*Wilson*, (bio of Woodrow Wilson), 1944.

*Wild in the Streets*, (What if the voting age were lowered to 14?), 1968 .

*Wilson*, (bio of Woodrow Wilson), 1944.

## MEDIA LITERACY

Center for Media Literacy. *Various teaching materials.* Los Angeles, CA: Center for Media Literacy.

Stauber, John. *Toxic Sludge Is Good for You.* Monroe, ME.: Common Courage, 1995.

## PERIODICALS

*Cartoon News*, New York City.

*George Magazine*, New York City.

*Brill's Content Magazine*, (media literacy & responsibility), NY.

*NewsCurrents* (Classroom Edition), Knowledge Unlimited, WI.

*react* magazine, Parade Communications, New York.

*Teen People*, People Magazine, New York

*TIME/Scholastic's Upfront*, Scholastic Publications, New York

*Wall Street Journal/Classroom Edition*, New York.

## POLITICS

*Fandex Family Field Guides (Presidents)*, New York: Workman Publishing, 1998.

Harlan, Judith. *Hispanic Voters: A Voice in American Politics.* New York: Franklin Watts, 1988.

Kronennwetter, Michael. *Politics and the Press.* New York: Franklin Watts, 1987.

Lindlop, Edmund. *Political Parties.* New York: Twenty-First Century Books, 1996.

Thomas, E.H. Gwynne. *Presidential Quiz Book*. New York: Hippocrene Books, 1988.

Weizmann, Daniel. *Take A Stand! Everything You Ever Wanted to Know About Government*. Los Angeles: Price Stern Sloan, Inc., 1996.

Zinn, Howard. *A People's History of the United States*. New York: HarperPerennial, 1995.

## R I G H T S

Franklin, Bob, ed. *The Handbook of Children's' Rights*. Routledge Press, 1995.

Jacobs, J.D. Thomas A. *What Are My Rights? 95 Questions & Answers about Teens and the Law*. MI: Free Spirit Publishing, 1997.

Kaufman, Gershen. *Stick Up for Yourself!: Every Kids' Guide to Personal Power & Self-esteem*. MN: Free Spirit Publishing, 1998.

Pascoe, Elaine. *Freedom of Expression: The Right to Speak Out IN America*. Brookfield CT, 1992.

Price, Janet R. *The Rights of Students: The Basic ACLU Guide To Student's Rights*. IL: Southern Illinois Univ. Press, 1998.

# Photo & Art Credits

# Index

*Sara Jane Boyers* is a former music industry attorney and
executive, and personal manager of performers. She changed direction to
write terrific books.

The creator of a popular series of illustrated books on contemporary
art & poetry, Ms. Boyers' first book, *Life Doesn't Frighten Me*, is an award-
winning pairing of the wildly expressive paintings of Jean-Michel Basquiat and
a stirring 1978 poem by Maya Angelou. Her second book, *O Beautiful for
Spacious Skies*, marries the whimsical paintings of Wayne Thiebaud to our
most famous hymn, "America the Beautiful", written by the leading woman
educator, poet & suffragette of the last century, Katharine Lee Bates.

Ms. Boyers' background in the music industry embarrasses her
teenagers because she is likely to start dancing and singing to the radio in
front of their friends. But it gave her a strong appreciation of the vitality and
creativity of youth that led her to write this book. The issues confronting
youth are numerous and she plans other books on this subject.

Sara Jane Boyers lives in Southern California with one husband,
two teens, three dogs, three cats, two guinea pigs, ten mice, many loud frogs,
Lester & Velvet the Chinchillas, two parakeets, one lovebird, Tucker the
caique, and several horses up the road. When she isn't working or feeding
animals, she photographs, art consults, actively speaks to schools and art
groups, rides horses and collects Twentieth Century art, weathervanes and toy
train signals.